SAC Time

A Navigator in the Strategic Air Command

Thomas E. Alexander

Edited by Dan K. Utley

Texas A&M University Press
College Station

Copyright © 2020 by Thomas E. Alexander and Dan K. Utley
All rights reserved

First edition

Library of Congress Cataloging-in-Publication Data

Names: Alexander, Thomas E., 1931– author. | Utley, Dan K., editor.
Title: SAC time : a navigator in the Strategic Air Command /
    Thomas E. Alexander ; edited by Dan K. Utley.
Other titles: Williams-Ford Texas A&M University military history series ;
    no. 165.
Description: First edition. | College Station : Texas A&M University Press,
    [2020] | Series: Williams-Ford Texas A&M University Military History
    series ; number 165 | Includes bibliographical references and index.
Identifiers: LCCN 2019047668 | ISBN 9781623498436 (hardcover) |
    ISBN 9781623498443 (ebook)
Subjects: LCSH: Alexander, Thomas E., 1931– | United States. Air Force.
    Strategic Air Command—Biography. | Flight navigators, Military—United
    States—Biography. | LCGFT: Biographies.
Classification: LCC UG626.2.A443 A3 2020 | DDC 358.40092 [B]—dc23
LC record available at https://lccn.loc.gov/2019047668

Dedicated to the spectacular lady who waltzed across Texas with me for twenty-five wondrous years. The dance has ended now, but my memories of it will never ever fade. Sleep well, Sweetheart!
Capy Stamps Alexander
1941–2018

∼

And to my friend Dan, who persuaded me to share these lofty tales from so very long ago.

Contents

Acknowledgments ix
Introduction xi
1. Securing the Skies 1
2. Getting Off the Ground 10
3. Sorting Them Out 22
4. From Mole Hole to Airborne 31
5. Fallout over Falun 40
6. A Stream and a Swagger 60
7. The Truth Was in the Stars 67
8. The Sheer Moment of Departure 76
9. Cuba 84
10. Flyover 91

Afterword: Around the Campfire 97
Dan K. Utley

Notes 103
Bibliography 105
Index 107

A gallery of photographs follow page 47.

Acknowledgments

My thanks for making this book a reality go out to Dan K. Utley, who could successfully do an oral history project with a grain of sand and make it sound like Mount Rushmore. My thanks also to his wife, Debby, who lent her inestimable talent to formatting and proofreading, and to Cynthia J. Beeman, who somehow managed to transcribe my usually mumbled words into understandable English. In the acquisition and collection of photos, I want to recognize Mr. Ben Guttery, Senior Program Manager of the Federal Aviation Administration. Ben is the consummate aviation historian whose enthusiastic support of this project resulted in important images that greatly enhance these memories. Special recognition goes to Dr. Jay Dew and Mr. Thom Lemmons, at Texas A&M University Press, who have been the conduits for both Dan and me to tell our stories of the military history of the Lone Star State. I must also acknowledge the late Gen. Curtis Emerson LeMay, who unknowingly set me on a true course to a wonderful life. Finally, here is an old air force guy's loving salute to my wife, Capy, without whom I would be nothing more than that mere grain of sand.

Introduction

The backstory of this memoir is good government—or at least the way government can work for the good of the people. Tom Alexander and I no doubt crossed paths at historical conferences in the 1990s; we both have vague memories of a handshake and hello at the 1998 Texas State Historical Association meeting in El Paso. Our first formal introduction occurred five years later, though, when he was appointed to the Texas Historical Commission (THC). In my capacity as assistant director of the agency's History Programs Division, I made a presentation at the new commissioner orientation in Kerrville. There Tom asked if we could have a meeting to discuss the agency's moribund military sites program, which had been without a staff leader for about a year. A few weeks later, he and I met for breakfast at his hotel in Austin. He had a coupon for a free muffin; I had nothing. After some pleasantries, he told me of his plan for a major initiative to commemorate the historical impact of World War II on Texas. I cautiously explained that our agency no longer had a military historian and that we had no budget for such an undertaking, to which he replied, "Well, OK, let's go ahead then."

As the planning began in the ensuing weeks, Tom and I had many occasions to visit again, but most notably in a series of one-on-one meetings at LBJ State Park, which we later referred to as the Stonewall meetings, given their proximity to the nearby town of the same name. At our very first meeting, per directions from my THC supervisors, I had to report to the new commissioner that his plans for the initiative might be too grand for our small agency and staff. Once again came the response, "Well, OK, let's go ahead then." With that admonition, various staff members embarked on a statewide plan that quickly raised about a million dollars in donations to fund oral history workshops, archeological surveys, special publications, museum exhibits, local history research, dozens of historical markers, and a memorable Capitol flyover of vintage aircraft, detailed in chapter 10 of this book.

Somewhere between the unshared muffin in Austin and the Stonewall meetings, Commissioner Alexander became one of my dearest friends. He was still my politically appointed boss, in effect, but he was also someone I greatly admired for his life experiences, his commitment to preserving the past, and his dry sense of humor. I remember distinctly when we were working on a promotional video for soliciting donations and he called and said, "For the background audio, I want the sound of a B-17 flying overhead and banking to the left." I agreed to the assignment without hesitation and waited a minute before calling him back. "I've got a recording of a B-17," I said, "but it's banking to the right." "Won't work," he replied before hanging up. That was my kind of humor. The fact that we mixed history and humor just made our visits more meaningful and enjoyable to me.

Tom and I visited a great deal between 2003 and 2005, when the THC kicked off the unprecedented initiative he had envisioned even before becoming a commissioner. As we traveled the state together and got to know each other better, he shared some of his military experiences with me. As a trained oral historian, they struck me as unique personal perspectives on the Cold War era, and I often thought about getting him to record some of his reminiscences for future researchers. Other assignments got in the way, including my transition to Texas State University and our shared work on several military history books. In the summer of 2016, though, he and I found time to conduct a series of interviews at his hilltop home in Kerrville about his service with the Strategic Air Command. Our mutual friend Cynthia J. Beeman, a former colleague at the THC, graciously provided the detailed transcripts that form the basis of this book. With those in hand, I began the careful editing process to transform the interview text into a narrative. My questions and comments have been removed, but Tom's words remain as spoken, helped only occasionally by segues and clarifications to close any undue gaps. The nature of oral history methodology is such that it does not always follow the historian's preferred chronology, so we made allowances for repeated stories and stories that spanned various sessions. The result is, we believe, a compelling account of one man's navigation through the Strategic Air Command in a time of national and personal uncertainty.

This is a single reminiscence of a chapter in military history lived out by what the author would quickly acknowledge is an ordinary man. As he wrote to remind me after seeing the original version of this introduction, "At no time during my years in uniform did I ever do anything that might be construed to be heroic, or brave, or courageous. All I did, man, was serve my country and fly around the world in those big, beautiful airplanes." While doing that, though, he also remembered events and people in detail. By reading Tom's firsthand accounts and memories of the past, readers will no doubt sense the tensions of the time and understand more about military perseverance and purpose, along with the intangible sense of flight that pervades the lives of those who have served in the air force and the air national guard. This is first-person history; this is oral history. The story of an ordinary individual in an extraordinary time has value for greater understanding of the human context. These are stories Tom Alexander waited much of his life to share with others, but they are as rich as the day they occurred. There are lessons here we all can learn about the personal military history of the Cold War era—and maybe even about the elements that form the basis of good government.

Dan K. Utley
March 2019

SAC Time

1
Securing the Skies

In the days and weeks immediately following the end of World War II, euphoria enveloped the citizenry of the victorious United States. Only a small number of those celebrating the victory already recognized that a new threat to the world peace so painfully just achieved was growing day by day. The eventual realization that the new potential enemy had just been America's ally during the war cast a long and ominous shadow over the hopes for a peaceful world, free of aggression. It soon became apparent to even the most optimistic pacifists that the Soviet Union, America's partner in victory, had become a belligerent seeker of new lands and the exponent of a political doctrine that held no regard for the human rights of either its own people or those of any other nation. Only such prescient leaders as Winston Churchill and the pugnacious American general George S. Patton had dared speak out previously against the tyranny of the Soviet leader, Josef Stalin, and the dangerous ambitions of his Communist government. Enigmatic, Stalin had a dark but still not as widely publicized reputation for being every bit as ruthlessly murderous as Germany's hated and deposed Adolf Hitler, architect of much of World War II.

Stalin's aggressive postwar occupation of the USSR's neighboring countries eventually proved blatant enough to cause the more liberal elements within the US government to join their conservative colleagues in recognizing the Soviet threat. The nation then began to prepare for yet another war, this time in reaction to the clear and present danger of a Soviet-inspired Communist plan to become the world's supreme nuclear superpower. An alarmed US leadership took its first and most significant step toward thwarting Soviet ambitions by creating the Strategic Air Command (SAC) on March 21, 1946, just six months after the formal surrender of Japan.

Headquartered at Bolling Field, in Washington, DC, the new organization came under the command of US Army Air Forces general George C. Kenney. During the war, Kenney held an unenviable and trying position as commander of Gen. Douglas MacArthur's air arm in the Southwest Pacific. Kenney's new command consisted mainly of units that managed to survive the army's massive and often mindless demobilization at the end of the war. Of the army air force's eighteen combat groups still operational in the fall of 1945, only two survived the drastic reduction of force. Initial units in the newly created command included those stationed at bases in Texas, New Mexico, Nebraska, Kansas, California, and Florida. Flying from those fields was a variety of war-tested aircraft, including the B-29 Superfortress; its cousin, the often cantankerous B-50; and briefly, fighter planes such as the P-47 and P-51. This rather ragtag assemblage of assorted, well-used aircraft seemed highly unlikely to carry out the command's mission statement as set forth by the US Army Air Force commanding general Carl Spaatz. The thrust of his statement read in part, "Be prepared to conduct long-range offensive operations in any part of the world, either independently or in cooperation with land and naval forces."

The new Strategic Air Command required most of the balance of 1946 and the first two months of 1947 to prove its aging inventory of aircraft was only marginally capable of accomplishing the goals set forth in the Spaatz mission statement. Further, the less than inspired leadership of George Kenney failed to provide adequate motivation for his command's efforts to attain those goals. Thomas M. Coffey, biographer of later SAC commander Curtis E. LeMay, attributed Kenney's lack of inspiration to his apparent greater interest in a projected United Nations position than his duties at SAC.

In September 1947, the United States Air Force (USAF) became an independent branch of military service. Less than a year later, USAF Headquarters relieved General Kenney of his command of SAC and ordered him to become commandant of the Air University at Maxwell Field in Alabama. To replace Kenney, the USAF named Lt. Gen. Curtis Emerson LeMay, its youngest three-star general (and soon to be four-star general) to assume command. At the same time, SAC moved its headquarters to Offutt AFB at Omaha, Nebraska, from Bolling Field, and far from the nation's capital and its political intrigue, which delighted LeMay. Apparently, a new commander and a new location seemed to be all the stimulants SAC needed to begin to flourish. The appointment of LeMay would likely have proven to be stimulus enough. His ironfisted, no-nonsense leadership quickly transformed SAC into arguably the most powerful military force in the world.

LeMay was to become the living persona of the elite outfit he commanded. Only forty-two years of age when he took charge, he was of the rare breed of general officers who reached the highest levels of star flag responsibility despite not being West Point graduates. Contrary to the army's traditional career path, LeMay earned his officer's commission through the Reserve Officers Training Corps (ROTC) at Ohio State University in 1928, following denial of his admission to the US Military Academy at West Point four years earlier. An honors graduate at Ohio State, LeMay received his commission in the US Army Reserve and began what proved to be a short-lived career as an engineer. His lifelong interest in flying soon prompted him to sign on as a cadet in the US Army Air Corps Flying School in 1930. His nearly uncanny proficiency as a pilot, and particularly as a navigator, fueled his rise to higher rank in a relatively short time span. That flying ability, his driving ambition, and his single-minded, almost ruthless, style of leadership brought him to the rank of major in 1941 during World War II, then lieutenant colonel in January 1942, full colonel just two months later, and then brigadier general in 1943 at the age of thirty-seven.

LeMay's remarkable success as a senior commander during World War II and his leadership of the 305th Bombardment Group in the European Theater brought him numerous decorations, along with a promotion to major general in 1944. He soon became commander of the newly formed Twentieth Air Force in the China-Burma-India Theater. His performance there brought about a position as chief of staff on Gen. Carl Spaatz's Strategic Forces, the forerunner of the Strategic Air Command he would someday take over. In addition, LeMay became the chief planning officer for all atomic bombing missions. Throughout his often-turbulent military career, LeMay practiced a cold, brutal, and merciless style of leadership. He seems to have been the philosophical heir to the unconditional warfare theory employed during the later stages of the Civil War by Gen. Ulysses S. Grant and his loyal lieutenant, William Tecumseh Sherman. In LeMay's mind, as in Grant's, no one and nothing were immune to the concept of unconditional total war. Some of LeMay's World War II contemporaries likely winced inwardly at his unauthorized decision to destroy the Japanese capital city of Tokyo through intensive and relentless firebombing in multiple raids that killed in one day nearly as many civilians as the later nuclear attacks on Hiroshima and Nagasaki. If such mass destruction of nonmilitary targets ever cost him even one sleepless night will never be known.

LeMay was not tall, but he was sturdy in physique. He walked at such a brisk pace that even younger officers had to trot just to keep up. He had a shock of dark hair and heavy jowls, and his mouth was set in a firm, stern expression with his lips turned down at the edges due to the early onset of a facial nerve disorder. The overall effect was that of a perpetual frown, usually beclouded by wreathes of tobacco smoke from at first a pipe and later his signature, ever-present cigar. The frown, heavy jowls, and ubiquitous cigar created a clear image of an intensely tough, driven, no mercy kind of general officer. The image was by no means a deception. He was therefore exactly the kind of leader SAC needed to ensure effective achievement of its global, pitiless mission.

Because of LeMay's relentless leadership, the United States attained the level of air superiority it required to curtail military air action by the increasingly aggressive Soviet Union. That undeniable superiority provided a clear advantage in the years following World War II, a period now known as the Cold War. The fundamental tenet of that undeclared conflict was the frightening concept of "mutually-assumed destruction," or MAD, an acronym seemingly appropriate for the effort. In the MAD scheme of things, America's putative enemy, the USSR, came to understand that any preemptive nuclear strike on the United States would trigger an instant reprisal by SAC, with its superior aircraft and more powerful nuclear weapons. An efficient early US warning system made it possible to detect the launching of any Soviet strike force in time for SAC planes to be airborne and on their way to selected targets, long before enemy planes had made it into American airspace. SAC had the will, the equipment, and the LeMay-inspired motivation to destroy its targets, and the Soviets knew it.

LeMay created SAC in his own image in a relatively short period. He placed trusted colleagues in key positions throughout his command and rewarded those who met or exceeded his lofty expectations with spot promotions and higher pay. Those who failed him, even slightly, faced summary dismissal without recourse. It was a "one-strike" ballgame played according to the most stringent rules imaginable. Firing by LeMay meant an instant reduction in rank, loss of pay, and reassignment to a less demanding and less rewarding position. Often, dismissal also led to an early retirement or at least little hope for any future promotion. To keep his command ready to take to the skies immediately, the general instituted an alert system. When on call, flight crews remained sequestered in underground quarters termed "mole holes" for obvious reasons. There the men ate and slept only a few steps away from their aircraft. Within minutes after the signal to scramble went out to the mole holes, the planes would be in the air, their weapons armed and ready to annihilate their targets. Later in the Cold War, SAC planes remained constantly aloft, with B-47s and tankers orbiting only hundreds of miles out of Soviet airspace and poised to attack. The airborne strike aircraft rotated to provide brief but adequate rest for crews and planes alike. At no time during the command's existence were the world's skies devoid of SAC aircraft.

Despite his impersonal businesslike approach in dealing with his subordinate officers, LeMay enjoyed their respect, for the most part. It is not possible to say his men loved him, but it is without doubt that they respected him. His officers, even though they clearly understood they could face dismissal and disgrace with a single flick of his wrist, remained exceptionally loyal to him. They were skilled warriors proud to be in the company of other men who, by the simple fact that they served in LeMay's command, were viewed with awe, pity, and great respect by other officers assigned to such earthbound duties as keeping good records in supply warehouses or processing incoming new recruits. As one observer put it, "Maybe SAC did not deserve such a purposeful and single-minded tyrant as Curtis LeMay, but no one could dispute that it needed him." Simply put, the Strategic Air Command and its tough commander seemed ideally suited for each other.

Under LeMay, SAC began to expand at an accelerated rate. Within a year of taking command, he persuaded USAF and congressional leaders to grow his command by an exceptional 70 percent. Ironically, the catalyst to this remarkable growth was SAC's specific and well-defined enemy, the USSR, with each aggression by the Soviets triggering an even more generous appropriation from Congress. Constant Soviet boasts about their ability to strike any target within the United States only created more funding from a Congress easily convinced by LeMay that his command and his command alone offered the only hope for salvation, should the Soviets' threatened Armageddon indeed come to pass. Because of its commander's constant push for even greater funding, SAC was soon able to divest itself of its initial fleet of battle-fatigued World War II–era aircraft. It quickly acquired more efficient long-range planes capable of meeting the initial Spaatz mission statement. The first wave of improved aircraft consisted of the often unreliable B-50 bombers, a modification of the war-tested B-29. Next came one of the world's most impressive bombers, the B-36 Peacemaker, with a wingspan of 230 feet. The model name reflected the LeMay-authored slogan for SAC: "Peace is our profession." Some wags saw fit to augment that slogan to read, "but war is our hobby," albeit then only out of the earshot of the commander.

Developed by Convair, the B-36 never flew "in anger" but was well equipped to do so, should the need arise. Eventually, SAC had at its disposal nearly five hundred of the massive giants, capable of carrying up to eighty-eight thousand pounds of bombs—more than any other aircraft before or since. In the memories of many, the sound of the Peacemaker remains unforgettable. Powered by six huge pusher engines mounted on the trailing edge of the wings, and eventually augmented by four jet engines, the aircraft produced a throbbing, pulsating drone clearly audible on the ground even before it flew overhead and long after it disappeared from view. At a low altitude, the noise was almost deafening, and even at twenty thousand to thirty thousand feet, the pulsing drone remained clear and distinctive. The passage of the giant at times seemed to block the sun from view—in effect, a manmade eclipse. Perhaps the Peacemaker's most significant claim to fame, aside from its bomb-carrying capacity and memory-haunting engine noise, was its ability to fly great distances without recourse to inflight aerial refueling, an untried procedure in 1948. In that year, for example, a B-36 flew nonstop from Carswell AFB in Texas to Hawaii and back, a distance of nearly nine thousand miles, in a record thirty-six hours. As crew members on B-36s liked to say, their planes landed only "so we could reenlist."

Record-breaking flights or not, the B-36, noisily plodding through American skies at all hours, soon fell victim to slowness—its only weakness. By the mid-1950s, the key words in the SAC lexicon had become *speed* and *mobility*. The B-36 could of course eventually reach its target and drop its enormous load of bombs, and it was certainly mobile enough to reach virtually any target in the world, but LeMay demanded more. SAC planes had to become faster and more capable of hitting any intercontinental target. Thus the Jet Age, the pinnacle of Cold War aircraft design achievement, came into being.

The most notable of the first generation of jet bombers was the Boeing B-47. Flown for the first time in late 1947, the plane was capable of attaining speeds of more than six hundred miles per hour, with a range of two thousand miles, carrying ten thousand pounds of bombs. Although the B-47 was superior to the B-36 in most respects, its operational range was not great enough to satisfy LeMay. His vision of maintaining an airborne strike force every minute of every day clearly hinged upon the range of his airplanes. The eventual solution to the challenge was aerial refueling, a technique not new in the mid-1940s but not yet thoroughly tested. LeMay eagerly seized upon the concept and pushed his airplane designers to deliver a "flying gas station"—aircraft capable of fueling SAC bombers while en route to their targets. Another cell of tankers, as they were dubbed, awaited the strike force on its way back to home base with much-needed fuel. The first tanker model to meet LeMay's expectations was the Boeing KC-97, essentially a modified C-97 Stratocruiser capable of offloading thousands of pounds of avgas to a bomber via an ingenuous flying boom device that protruded from the rear of the tanker, a mere thirteen feet from the fuel tank, located on the fuselage of the bomber. The in-air refueling concept placed new emphasis on the "strategic" part of the command's name. Eventually, with nearly nine hundred tankers and more than two thousand of the B-47 swift jet bombers that could safely strike any target anywhere in the world, Carl Spaatz's original SAC mission statement had been attained at last.

There was, however, one serious problem yet to be solved—namely, the vast airspeed disparity between the tanker, with a top speed of 375 mph, and the slowest speed at which a B-47 could safely fly without stalling, approximately 400 mph. As a result of this disparity, during the critical hookup stage of the refueling process, during which the boom was inserted into the B-47, the KC-97 was flying at full throttle just to maintain its 375 mph speed while the receiver vessel (the B-47) wallowed behind, barely able to stay aloft at such a slow speed. The obvious options to this dangerous problem were to either develop a faster tanker or quickly create a new, slower jet bomber. Those who knew LeMay even slightly would have realized that a faster tanker would be the option he preferred. The result was the KC-135, a derivative of the Boeing 707 transport plane. The new aircraft could maintain a top speed of nearly 600 mph, quite compatible with that of the B-47. Nearly eight hundred of the KC-135 tankers were thus in service by 1964. With this winning combination of aircraft finally in place, LeMay seemed satisfied, but only for a moment. He was constantly lobbying his superiors at USAF Headquarters to provide him with even more aircraft, as well as urging airplane designers to develop even faster bombers.

In the mid-1950s, what proved later to be a flawed intelligence report that the Soviet Air Force was superior to SAC in both quantity and quality of aircraft prompted Pres. Dwight Eisenhower to demand greater improvements in LeMay's inventory. The result was a burst of growth in not only machines but workforce. In 1953, for example, the USAF had 170,000 personnel, with 19,994 officers. The Eisenhower directive raised the total personnel count to 258,703 personnel and 35,000 officers within a five-year period. Total US military strength grew from 387,000 in 1948 to 983,000 by 1952, due to Cold War pressures. During that time frame, nearly every new officer coming into the USAF through the cadet program, enlistments, or the ROTC were more or less gang-pressed into the Strategic Air Command.

To those who view LeMay through a modern day prism of political correctness, he is a loathsome, perhaps even murderous, mad tyrant. What else is there to think of a general capable of boasting of his firebombing of Tokyo, "We roasted, baked, or broiled 100,000 Japs today"? Or one who suggested the only way to deal with the North Vietnamese was "to nuke them back into the Stone Age"? However, to those who still remembered Pearl Harbor and the fear and anger that seized the US following the attack and to those who built bomb shelters in their backyards to be prepared when the Russians came, LeMay was something of a knight in shining armor. No matter that he had killed all of those Japanese to retaliate for Pearl Harbor—he was now holding the Soviets at bay. To many, he was an avenging angel.

For those who served in his command, Curtis LeMay was a taskmaster, a perfectionist, and more than a little bit frightening. When word spread that "The General" was on the base, officers and enlisted men alike stood a bit taller and made certain their uniform neckties were straight and hats worn precisely according to regulations. Those who actually saw him can recall the sudden thrill that ran through them. There in person was the man who could in a flash either give them a promotion or return them to kitchen police duty. Mainly, though, there was the heroic zealot who had saved America from total destruction. I had the opportunity to see LeMay in action, and I remember those feelings well, more than a half century after they first crossed my mind as a part of the greater command.

This then is my personal perspective of that story, as one who gratefully served under LeMay's command, observed his successes closely, and worked diligently to further his goals and objectives for SAC. I did so willingly, although I was admittedly a low man in the rigid chain of command in the 1950s—one of twenty thousand new officers ordered into service in 1953. Regardless, I offer these oral history memoirs of my "SAC time" as a means of complementing and honoring the recorded stories of others—especially those who navigated the skies in a time of national and global uncertainty. Additionally, however, I hope these stories provide an honest and reflective account of the impact the Cold War had on individuals who were then on the front lines of defense—like it or not.

2
Getting Off the Ground

I was born in Long Beach, California, on July 11, 1931, in the early years of the Great Depression. My father, Edward Clifton Alexander, was a stockbroker and a native of Rio Vista, Texas, in Johnson County, south of Cleburne. My mother, Ruth Ethlyn (nee Massey), was (I suppose) a professional sorority girl, as she was the president of the Pi Beta Phi sorority in Los Angeles. She was born in Topeka, Kansas, in 1898, the same year as my father, although she was a couple of months older. At the time they met, he worked in a bank in Wellington, Kansas, south of Wichita, and she was living nearby with her family. My dad was not the most gregarious person in the world, but somehow, she saw something in him that she liked, obviously, and they got married and had two sons. My brother, Richard "Dick" Alexander, served in World War II with the US Navy in the Pacific. I like to say he worked for Adm. Chester Nimitz, and somewhere down the line, you could say that might be true. Although Dad's sons both had military careers, he was not a military man himself, and in fact, I think he went out of his way not to be. He often told a story that I think was probably apocryphal: He alleged to have wanted to join the US Army Signal Corps back in the early days of World War I, when he would have been about seventeen or eighteen years old. He said he volunteered for that service and received his acceptance notice, but somehow his mother intervened and decided he should not go. I am uncertain if that prevailed in World War I or not, but it would not have worked in World War II. According to his story, though, she convinced somebody (theoretically—let me put it that way), and he did not go. He was always, I think, rather apologetic about the fact he was never in the service, especially, perhaps, because his sons were. He never said anything to that effect, though.

Thinking of my father's personality, I believe it was his unsociability that resonated most in me. He could charm a bird out of a tree if he wanted to, but the older he got, the more withdrawn he became. He was not that actively engaged as a father, or later as a grandfather, and lived a great deal within himself. I always thought he was totally dedicated to my mother, and they were together for fifty-five years. Despite their closeness, she did manage to play one significant trick on him, and she did not share the deception with me until after his funeral service. My brother and I took her to a bar—a place up in Woodland Park, Colorado—and that was an acceptable way of celebrating funerals in that particular place. She was very fond of alcoholic beverages by this time, when she was in her eighties. We were sitting at the bar and she started to laugh, which seemed rather unusual, given that she had just buried her husband with a full Eastern-Star Masonic ceremony and all that. I asked, "What in the world is so funny?" She replied, "You know, for fifty-five years I fooled that man every morning of every day." I was caught off guard. "What in the world did you do?" "Well," she chuckled, "he thought if an egg was not bright yellow, it wasn't fresh, so I put yellow food coloring in his scrambled eggs every morning, and he never knew it. And I was always afraid when he was dying," she added, somewhat modestly, "I was afraid I was going to tell him, but I never did. We would go on trips to restaurants, and he would order eggs and then send them back because he felt they were not fresh, even when the waiter assured him that chickens had laid them that very morning. Unless they were *amarilla*, really bright yellow, he wasn't going to have anything to do with them."

My mother was a charming lady—very charming—as all mothers are, I guess, to their sons. She was certainly a great influence on my life, probably more so than my father. Not long after I was born in Long Beach, my dad moved the family back to Kansas, as selling stocks and bonds in Los Angeles during the Depression was not promising work. This ability to relocate thus became very important to me, and I developed a transportable sense of place as a result. Although Dad was a Texan by birth, he was part of a family that had also moved quite a bit. His father, Ireanus "Rene" Morse Alexander, was a grain elevator operator in Rio Vista, but he had a solid southern pedigree. He was one of about ten sons, and his grandfather had served in the Revolutionary War and ridden with Light Horse Harry Lee in the First Virginia Volunteers. Because of that, Dad was active in the Sons of the American Revolution (SAR). The family came from a little town called Marrowbone, in southern Kentucky. My family returned there for a funeral one time, and I remember the cemetery filled with Alexander graves. It seemed like every one of them bore a Daughters of the American Revolution (DAR) marker. The senior Alexander in all this, John Alexander, called himself "Sergeant." While military monikers were more numerous back then, often representing a personally elevated rank of service, it turns out the good sergeant had actually been a captain in the cavalry. I'm not sure why he chose to demote himself instead.

While thinking about the influential family members in my life, I should note the role of my maternal grandmother. I am not really sure of her name, because she changed it with great regularity, marrying three times. It was probably and officially something like Mary Ann Hastings Massey. Her maiden name was Hastings, and then she married a guy who was a farrier, and he was a sulky driver as well, and a racer. I have the diamond stick pin from his necktie and cravat. They divorced somewhere along the way, after my mother was born. I never knew the man; he went to California and is buried out there.

My grandmother was a beautiful woman who looked like a Gibson Girl. She had the hourglass figure and always wore big hats. She worked for a while as a cook on a ranch. She was amazing in the kitchen and prepared food by the pinch and dab method, never using a measuring cup. I lived with her for a considerable period of time, and she was an absolute character. I do not believe she ever told the truth in her life. She would tell me that she was born in Chillicothe, Missouri, and that she saw Jesse James. Her father ran a boarding house somewhere in Missouri, and she remembered that her father told her that Jesse James and his brother were coming to the boarding house, so she had to hide. She hid under the stairs, but they were open, so she could see what was taking place. I said, "What do you remember about Jesse James?" And she said, "His boots. I could see his boots going up those stairs." She would then weave this amazing story, and she really impressed me in that regard, but maybe I am a bit more truthful than she was. She loved to drink beer, but Kansas was bone dry in those days. When I was five years old, she took me to a "watering hole," and how in the world they were selling beer I have no idea. I had a little tiny glass mug that had the name Coors on it, and she would order her beer and pour off the foam into my little glass. I would drink that, and the waitress would come by and say, "We can't sell alcohol to minors." Grandmother would say, "I'm just giving him the foam. That's not beer." I can honestly say I've been drinking beer for eighty years, because I started when I was five.

Grandmother was, in reality, quite loving and understanding, and she spoiled me rotten. Whatever I wanted, she would give me. Her second husband, or third maybe, was a road foreman for engines of the Atchison, Topeka, and Santa Fe Railway, and out of that came my affiliation and tremendous love of railroading. When he would pack his grip—his suitcase—he would include a pint of bourbon whiskey that he purchased from some bootlegger. When I asked what it was, he would say, "That's my medicine," and then he would fold up that grip and head out in his bib overalls, shirt, tie, and fedora hat. He was the foreman, and all the engineers reported to him. Occasionally, when he wanted to go back to driving a locomotive, he would do that, and he would get a message to my grandmother that he was coming into town. When he did, we would go down to the depot and watch the engine come in, and he would signal with the whistle when he got close. He had his own style of whistle-blowing; he would come into town with that thing blaring and him waving out of the cab, and her heart would just melt. Man, that was the greatest thing she ever saw.

The Alexander family lineage beyond Kentucky includes connections to Sir William Alexander, Lord Chancellor to King James VI of Scotland (later James I of Great Britain). In return for his service to the crown, William Alexander received a place called Novia Scotia. From there, his son came to the United States and founded Alexandria, Virginia. My brother and I went to Scotland for genealogical research on the Alexanders, who were originally MacAlesters (son of Alexander) and who lived on the Kintyre Peninsula along the Carryover Canal, which dates to about 1100 CE. In our search, we ended up seeking out the family historian, Gretchen Alexander, who lived in the ancestral home that still bore the crest above the door. That just impressed my mother to no end, because she loved that she had married somebody historically legitimate.

My father worked hard throughout his life. He went from brokering and banking into real estate in Colorado, although he did not push the latter pursuit as much as he might have. It was while in Pueblo, though, that we first learned about the US entry into what would be World War II. Dick and I had gone to the movies on Sunday, December 7. I was ten and he was fifteen, and for decades we have argued over which movie we saw that day. He has always maintained it was *Ten Gentlemen from West Point*, while I stubbornly insisted it was *My Favorite Blonde*, but recent research for this book now conclusively proves we were both wrong, since neither movie debuted until the following year. Regardless that detail, we know that we first heard about the Japanese attack while riding the streetcar back home. There was a kid on a corner selling an extra edition of the *Pueblo Chieftain*, and the big headline literally said, "Extra! Extra! Pearl Harbor Attack!" Everyone on the streetcar wanted one, and out of the ten people on that streetcar, I doubt if any knew where Pearl Harbor was or why there was a war. I mean, nobody followed that. The general view was that we knew we were going to get involved in the war, but nobody followed it at the time. Dick, being fifteen, realized, "Uh-oh, the writing is pretty much on the wall and I'm going to be going to this thing pretty quickly." As it turns out, he had a few years to wait. He graduated from high school on D-Day, June 6, 1944, and went the next day to enlist in the navy. He did not need parental consent, which Mother would likely not have provided, as she was rather possessive. Regardless, he joined the navy and received orders to Cour d'Alene, Idaho, which is not the first place one thinks of in terms of naval training.

After Dick left for the service, I would read the newspapers every day, and I just absorbed the war news. I think that has influenced me all my life. Soon enough, I knew I wanted to be a marine. I must have been out of my mind, but I wanted to be a marine. I convinced my mother to make some chevrons for me that she sewed out of remnants—little pieces of cloth that nobody wanted. She thus made me a sergeant major in the US Marine Corps, and I put that on a jacket and, boy, all the kids were impressed. Instead of playing cowboys and Indians, we played—pardon the expression—soldiers and Japs. And that was it. Political correctness did not exist much in 1944. The Japanese were always the villains and the American soldiers were always the good guys. Even then, on make-believe battlefields, there was never any question in my mind—I was going to go into the military. There was definitely a kick-ass mentality at the time. I remember thinking, *I'm going to kill those guys. How dare they attack Pearl Harbor and kill all those people?* That was a singular event, and it influenced seemingly everybody in this country to hate the Japanese.

If you look at the publications of the time, there was so much fervor, but also so much bad information. I remember a *Life Magazine* article on how to tell the difference between the Japanese and the Chinese. It was totally erroneous stuff, like "You'll know the Japanese because the big toe and the next toe to it are separated from years of wearing sandals." The cultural differences were engrained in us, and as a military man, the memories of those days still linger with me, and I carry some resentments. I resent how history has changed through the years—something I experienced when serving as an advisor to the Museum of the Pacific War in Fredericksburg, Texas. As part of that team, I had to remind some of my younger colleagues about the nature of the conflict, the reasons why we entered, and the fact that we were the victors. They believed we should not have dropped the atomic bombs that resulted in so many deaths, but as Curtis LeMay once famously said, "There were no innocent civilians." He was the overall commander of that US Air Force that dropped those weapons, but he believed it just had to be done. It saved literally countless lives, and we will never know the magnitude of those the bombs spared. The alternative, in hindsight—the invasion of Japan—would have been far worse. It was a war, and as LeMay knew, if you are going to enter a war to kill someone, you simply have to kill them. It is a tremendous attitude, I believe, that does not exist today.

Not long after the war began, we returned to Wellington, which was a typical midwestern agricultural town of that era. It had a population of about 7,500 at the time, but with little diversity. There was one Hispanic kid in my class and maybe one African American kid as well, but I am not sure. In many respects, it was like a Norman Rockwell setting, with everything as it should be, except that a war was going on overseas and residents were concerned if their loved ones in the service would return—and, if so, what condition they would be in. At the time, though, communication was not as it is today, so there was this pervasive fear and dread of not getting updated news from the fronts for long periods of time. Not hearing was the hardest part sometimes. I never saw my father show any emotion until the war ended, but then he broke. We were fortunate that Dick eventually returned unharmed.

During those war years, when business was once again difficult, Dad took a job working for Boeing in Wichita, thirty-two miles away from where lived in Wellington. He became a buying agent for the manufacturing company with no qualifications at all, and as part of his area he traveled back into Texas. I remember he once told me about purchasing a piece of costume jewelry at Neiman Marcus for mother that she particularly liked. Little did I realize that I would someday end up working for that great company.

Wichita boomed during the war years. At one point, Beechcraft, Cessna, and Boeing were all operating out of there. We finally moved there because the commute was tough for Dad and gasoline was hard to come by, and there was a thirty-five-mile-per-hour speed limit. I really do not know how Dad got the job at Boeing, because he had no training in buying anything for airplanes. He was something of a con man, I guess, and maybe I resemble him in that regard—I have been told that, at least. Regardless of my father's credentials, however, B-29s ended up flying around with parts he bought for their production.

One thing in particular about my Wichita stint was how, as a Boy Scout (Flaming Arrow Patrol of Troop 22), I participated in a war bond drive. To raise money for the bonds, the Scouts went door to door, selling packs and cartons of cigarettes. I was thirteen or fourteen at the time. That would no doubt be newsworthy these days. The town was just exploding with people, given the wartime production at the aircraft companies. The population went from around fifty thousand to more than a hundred thousand in about a year. I remember the widespread patriotism of that time and place. It was a "just" war, we believed, and everyone understood that and accepted it. There was no quibbling about the nation's involvement. We had been attacked and we struck back, and even liberals understood that. It was a very simple arrangement. It seemed to me that almost every house had a service flag in a window, and there was rationing, some of which was of negligible help to the war effort.

Some of the various home front programs went unheeded, particularly in the small towns. You know, about halfway through the war, the government announced a need for meatless Tuesdays, but it absolutely set the country on its ear, because who was the government to tell individuals they could not eat meat on Tuesdays? The general response was something along the lines of, "We'll have meat seven days a week, by God!" You know, in little towns like that, residents could just go out in the country and cut a deal with a farmer for their own supply of meat. Scrap drives, though, were different, and there was widespread participation for those. I can remember when I was at school in Pueblo, Colorado, there were metal scrap drives that included automobile chassis, which must have been dragged there by kids. And then there were rubber drives, to which patriotic women contributed their girdles. I used to play basketball on the playground where there was a whole stack of rubberized lingerie laying out there in the rain. I do not believe anyone ever picked them up, and maybe it is still there underground as part of some strange archeological feature.

The town had cooking fat drives, and I remember taking coffee cans full of bacon grease and putting them on a pile in the schoolyard. The place looked like a junkyard, with all sorts of debris, from rusted tractors to mounds of rubber tires. The mess stayed there a long time and may never have been utilized for the war effort, but it was a symbol of patriotism, nonetheless. It made us feel like we were doing our part to help the troops, like my brother.

Dick was my hero, and I enjoyed following in his wake. He had been a signal corpsman on a landing craft (LST) and was in the Pacific at the time of the atomic bombs at the end of the war. His letters home influenced me a lot. Those that made it through the censors would have comments about Hawaii and other exotic locales, and I tracked his movements using pins I stuck in a large world map. I was five years younger than Dick and thought he was the greatest person who ever lived, so I was punching these pins all around the Pacific, until all of a sudden in the mid-Pacific the detailed information stopped because the censors had stepped in to do their jobs. He has always told me that he was on his way to the invasion of Japan, because his ship was carrying tanks, when the air force came and ended the war, essentially. Consequently, his ship turned around and went back, avoiding additional combat, and he has always appreciated my association with the air force because of that. He did not enjoy his service and for a long time would not talk about those years. Finally, though, over beers, he loosened up and said, "I just couldn't stand all that—somebody telling me what to do." I was the opposite, though, because I liked and appreciated the discipline of the military.

I vividly remember the circumstances of his homecoming. When he knew he was headed back, he sent a message, so we were expecting him. He had been promoted and was a Signalman Third Class by the time he left the service. He came back home on a train, and the Wellington High School band, which included me as a trumpeter, was there at the Santa Fe depot to welcome that particular trainload. We welcomed a lot of trains in those days, appropriately, by playing "The Stars and Stripes Forever," John Philip Sousa's rousing patriotic march of the 1890s. There were always large crowds of people, and one thing that was so fascinating about the homecomings for me was the routine. The trains would come into the depot and the guys would get off, still in their uniforms and carrying their duffel bags. Up front, out of the baggage car, came coffin after coffin after coffin, and that little town likely suffered more losses per capita than many others in the war. It seemed like almost everybody had a son who died in the war somehow. Dick returned safely, though, but he was not the same brother I had known before the war. I think it was probably endemic the way his attitude toward life had changed completely. He was surly and did not know what to do. He did not want to go back into the service, but he also had no plans to return to civilian life. Somehow, as a result, he and my father clashed. My father was, after all, the authority symbol, and Dick was shying away from that authority and had just walked away from several years of it in military life. The result was they almost became alienated. Dick would go down to the American Legion hall and come home fairly "beered up" at night. Pretty soon he thought, "I can't do this," so he went off to school at Kansas State College in Manhattan. He and Dad finally got together and all that, but I think the homecoming was traumatic for all of us, because people sat around and worried about him, and then there he was but he was not the same guy.

That same change was also evident in others who came back from the war. One I remember was a great big guy named Duely Sharpsteen, who came back to Wellington High School after serving as a marine in the South Pacific. Duely would fight anybody, and he had a lot of anger. He had come back to this dinky little Kansas town to its dinky little high school and was playing football not long after fighting on the battlefield. Weighing in at 133 pounds, I was cannon fodder playing football out there, always assigned to the second team. I would get down face-to-face with this giant, who was 6'5" and weighed 225 pounds. There I was with my skinny legs and an ill-fitting helmet, and I had to take on Duely Sharpsteen. I was playing end at the time, and once in position he would say something like, "Tom, how's your grandmother?" And I'd say, "Oh, she's doing OK, Duely." Then—*wham!* He would hit me, and I would go flying off into outer space. My 133 pounds could not stop 225 pounds of well-conditioned, ex-marine muscle.

Shortly after my graduation from Wellington High School in 1949, I too headed off to Kansas State. Dick had joined a fraternity when he was there and enjoyed the camaraderie, so I went up there as a legacy candidate and was accepted into the same frat. Kansas State was a land-grant college and ROTC was mandatory, except for veterans, so I followed a different course from Dick in that regard. I started my military training in antiaircraft artillery and was pleased with that mission. Overall, in Kansas as well as across the nation, it was an uneasy time. Millions of young men and women returned home, and every last one had changed to some significant degree. That was the setting in which I sought my degree, basing my initial plan on my high aptitude in history and political science, and the study of military affairs. The ROTC was equally important to me and was an integral part of campus life, given that it was a requisite course for male students. As a freshman, I got to thinking, "This outfit needs some music," so

I founded a drum and bugle corps, which is still in existence. Every Thursday the corps would march past the reviewing stand and form right in front of the commandant. We would lead off with some stirring march while everybody else marched by. We probably had ten bugles and as many drums. I would arrange what we were going to play, and we would rehearse on Wednesday nights. They guys loved it, because they got to wear lanyards and all this kind of stuff.

It was a great experience in Manhattan overall, and I would have finished at Kansas State, but there was a beautiful girl whose father was a colonel at Fort Riley. (I realize this makes me sound like a real creep.) Here I am, a sophomore second lieutenant cadet in the ROTC, and she was a junior, I think. Her name was Barbara Ford, and I thought, "I'm going to marry Barbara Ford, and I'm going to join the army. I'm going to go right to the top because her daddy's a big-time guy." So, we dated seriously, and I really thought I was going to marry her. I was probably nineteen years old. I had a date with her one night, though, and she said, "Tom, I'm getting married." She married a captain, who had the same idea I did, but he was Regular Army and I was ROTC. So that took care of that. I was just heartbroken, and at that time, my parents were going to move to Colorado, to Woodland Park, where they retired. I had always admired the University of Colorado—just the way it looked, a beautiful campus in that beautiful city of Boulder. So I went up there when they moved and got admitted as a junior transfer into prelaw at the university. My degree plan was disguised as political science, but it evidently counted as prelaw. Coincidentally, the university had just started an air force ROTC program, which I joined, moving from artillery gunner in Kansas to airman basic in Colorado. While I had enjoyed the experience of working with artillery at Fort Riley, I looked forward to flying for a change.

I remember my first flight had been in Pueblo, Colorado, and I was about six years old at the time. My dad took my brother and me out to the airport, and I recall this quite clearly. My mother had gone to the ladies' room at the airport, and she came out and said, "Where are the boys?" And Dad looked up to the sky and said, "There they go." He had booked us on a little Piper Cub, or maybe it was bigger than that, because both of us were in there. We just circled the field, flew around, and looked down at the airfield. Mother said to my dad, "How did you do that? For heaven's sake!" Regardless her concern, I am glad it worked out, because that was my very first flight—probably about seventy-nine years ago.

What I liked most about flight, I think, was just getting off the earth. There is an inspirational poem about aviation by John Gillespie Magee Jr., called "High Flight," which includes the memorable line, "Oh, I have slipped the surly bonds of earth, and danced the skies on laughter-silver wings." I do not believe there was ever an air force guy who could not subscribe to that. Not that life on earth is undesirable—there is just something about flight that is so compelling, and getting on that plane is magical. I tried to be a pilot, but I was not eligible at that point because my eyes were bad. They are OK now, but I could not see well enough then. Pilots had to have 20/20 uncorrected vision in those days, although now it is maybe 20/80. Since I failed to make the cut as a pilot, I decided I would go to the navigation school instead. I wanted to go on flying status, whatever it was, whatever it took to fly in airplanes, and that was the only way to go, so that is what I signed up for.

Coming out of ROTC, I had several options, although it was obligatory federal service at that point. After a student collected that money for school, he could go into operational aircraft or into administration, logistics, and fields like that, which bored me to no end. I just had to fly, and I would have flown in a Piper Cub just to get up in the air. I will never forget it; it still is a lasting memory to me how great it was—to the point that I sometimes regret ever getting out. I just really wish I had stayed in the service. During my ROTC training, we flew in B-25 Mitchell bombers stationed at Lowry Field in Denver. The B-25s had to have been the loudest airplanes on the inside. We had to wear headsets to even think straight. That also, I believe, contributed to my Veterans Administration supply of hearing aids. It was just *bam, bam, bam*, constantly, and after we flew for five or six hours in that thing, we were almost deaf. Despite that, I was finally doing what I felt called to do, and that was to fly.

3

Sorting Them Out

I graduated from the University of Colorado on June 6, 1953. I did not wear a cap and gown at the ceremony, though, because the US Air Force ROTC cadets graduated in khakis. We had no aeronautical rating, obviously, but we received our second lieutenant bars as part of the event that day. We graduated in Folsom Stadium in Boulder and were individually called up to receive our degrees and then our bars from the commandant. A curious thing is that I remember it being a beautiful day, but about fifty years later I read that that day was the last recorded historical snowfall at Boulder, and it snowed ten inches. I don't remember that at all, because I was so happy about getting that degree and getting those bars. I remember that among all the sergeants in the ROTC, it was a tradition that the first guy who saluted you once you had your commission got a dollar bill, and so we walked off the steps and all these guys were lined up, ready to salute. We were all forewarned about this, so I had a dollar in my pocket and just handed it to the first guy.

Even though I was elated at the prospects represented by that day, I think my father was terrified about what it meant and my mother was probably even more so. I had constantly expressed this overwhelming desire to fly, but I guess this news alarmed them because it seemed to me that every time a plane crashed somewhere, the newspapers were putting every crash that occurred anyplace in the world on the same day on the front page, so it looked like every plane was falling out of the sky. I think my mother, therefore, thought that every plane I was on was going to be lost. Every time I left it was very emotional. With fresh memories of worrying about my brother during the war, they quite understandably could not stand the thought of dealing with those emotions again.

I think my brother liked the idea of my flight service in the military. I think he carried the same militaristic feelings that I have toward things, which is not to go out and kill somebody unnecessarily, but just to be ready to do so. Unlike him, though, I liked the discipline of the service. Quite frankly, I think that was probably what attracted me more than anything else—the fact if you said you were going to be somewhere at 07:45, you had better be there at 07:44. Since those days, a guiding principal for me has been "if you're on time, you're late." It made such a lasting impression on me to maintain personal discipline. It removes a lot of worry and confusion in an individual's life, and there are fewer doubts.

Leading up to eventual graduation, the ROTC class out of Colorado had summer camp at Clovis Air Force Base in New Mexico in July, and air-conditioning was unheard of. Corps leaders announced a program whereby they were going to choose six cadets out of the mass of young people down there for summer camp between their junior and senior years. They were going to pick six outstanding cadets to go to a firepower demonstration at Eglin Field in Florida. I had heard about that and really wanted to go see it, but it was not my intent, I guess. To get to the mess hall at Clovis, you had to walk directly past the administration building. Rather than march, we just walked over, and while going over there to have lunch or dinner, if I saw a piece of paper on the ground, I would pick it up and throw it in the rubbish bin. Somebody was watching this, I guess, and I was named one of those six outstanding cadets, in part because of the fact that I was so tidy.

We also had to lead a formation in drill periodically, and I had read about a formation called "To the Winds March," and you would march along and say, "To the four winds, harch!" The first guy, the first rank, would then keep going straight, the second rank would turn off to the left, the third rank would turn off to the right. Instead of just splitting, one guy would turn around the other way, and if you kept your cadence long enough and just kept barking this cadence, they would all come back together. This could be a bit tricky, because they are going away from the sound, but I had a pretty good voice and could shout out those commands. At the reviews I would proudly show off my "To the Winds March" directions. We would rehearse this, and these guys would all come back, and afterward the colonel would say, "How'd you do that?" He was impressed with the precision, which was not necessarily the norm. There was a gentleman once who, as a cadet, let a formation get out of control, and he marched them right through the commanding officer's front yard, which the commander's wife had just irrigated, and these guys marched and trampled on through. They were not about to stop until ordered to do so, and this guy just panicked. "I can't stop them!" he yelled, but to no avail. They could have just marched all the way back to Colorado, I guess.

Upon graduation from the university, I received orders to report on my birthday, July 11, to Ellington Field near Houston for basic training in navigation. Ellington was an interesting base. It was hot, terribly hot, in July along the Texas gulf coast. As one might imagine, humidity was often close to 100 percent. I checked in and the clerk said, "We've had a little holdup on the class ahead of you. The weather's been so bad that we could not fly all the required hours, so we want you to take time off." He added, "Just take a week. We're delayed by a week. Come back on the eighteenth." I respectfully said OK. I was by myself and had a car. I was getting money, paid by the government, but I was in a place I knew nothing about. I asked the clerk what I should do, and he replied, "Have you ever seen the ocean?" I said, "No, I was born in a hospital by it, but I've never seen it." "So why don't you go down to Galveston? It's only about sixteen miles away," although there was no freeway at the time. "Go down there and just enjoy it," he directed. "Sit on the beach and do what you want to do on the beach." He said, "Before you go, here's a book I have to give you. This is a book of off-limits institutions in Galveston, Texas." I said, "What do you mean?" He explained, "These are whorehouses and illegal bars and things like that. Don't go there, because the air police are all over the place, and they're looking for guys that come down there out of Ellington so they can give them a hard time." Well, that book became a sort of unofficial travel guide. With it in hand, I got into in my little two-color Ford special and went down to Galveston. I just could not believe it, you know. I thought, "What a wonderful thing—and at the government's expense."

Galveston was a wide-open town then regarding vices. The Maceo brothers and others just defied the law. You could go down there to that big gambling pier, and when they heard that a raid was coming, the employees would dump all their machines and gambling paraphernalia off the end into the water, making it difficult to be caught. After the police raiders left, so the stories go, the workers would dredge up the machines and start all over. I had never seen anything like this, you know, in Kansas or Colorado. Man, this was a different thing. Pretty soon a bunch of us trainees identified each other and shared quite a bit of time together following the government-provided travel guide. We never saw an air policeman, perhaps because they were so busy elsewhere. Galveston was said to be, at the time, as corrupt, illegal, or decadent as any city in the world. Reportedly, Shanghai was number one and Galveston was number three. You would have thought that Texas was an absolute fountain of bourbon and beer and whatever. No prohibition.[1]

Thankfully, I survived the week in Galveston and made my way back to Ellington. I got into active duty and started with the C-47—a cargo plane known as the Gooney Bird. It was a taildragger DC-3, and to get in the thing you had to almost be an acrobat. It was all decked out in navigation training equipment, and it was a terrifically reliable aircraft that is still flying, although the prototype dated to 1927. It was a supply plane, and paratroopers used them in World War II. They were ideal for troop transport because you could pack a lot of guys in and get them from point A to point B efficiently. It was great fun to train on the Gooney Bird. From that model, though, we went to the much more desirable Convair T-29, called the Flying Classroom, and it was just completely packed. Every station had a complete navigation system, radar set, and every kind of device one needed to navigate an aircraft. I also flew aboard B-25s during active duty training, and then, after getting my wings, I advanced to the Boeing KC-97 tanker known as the Stratocruiser. It was made up of B-50 fuselages, one set on top of the other, which does not sound pretty, but it worked. I also flew for a while on the B-47. I think my favorite plane, though, was the B-25, because the navigator sat up in the bombardier's compartment and could easily access the radar. I was eventually triple-rated as a navigator, bombardier, and radar bombardier. The technology evolved quickly, and some bombers (designated by B) gave way to reconnaissance bombers (RB), with the first one being the B-36. Pretty soon, all these appellations—36, 47, and 52—lined up, because it was evolving so rapidly that nobody knew what was going to be the plane you would be in by the time you got out.

In the Reconnaissance B-25, stationed in Ellington Field in Houston, we would fly over the entire state of Texas, and there was a great big open hole in the back of the plane, with a camera mount for photo reconnaissance. I would take long strip pictures of a specified area, like Navasota in Grimes County, which was one of our favorite targets, as were the marshaling yards of the railroad in Fort Worth. One time when we flew over Navasota, I had an orange in my pocket, and when I leaned over to look out the hole, out it went. I always wondered what people down there in Grimes County thought of the flying orange. One time I dropped a watch out that same hole and had to explain where that went in flight, as it was about a four-hundred-dollar, GI-issue Master watch.

As a second lieutenant right out of college, I started at the bottom of the barrel. In fact, the first day I got there, before we figured out that I was going to have to wait, the adjutant came in and I saluted. You are supposed to salute the adjutant when you check in on a base, but this guy kind of looked at me like, "What the hell are you doing?" The air force was not very strict on discipline—at that level, anyway. But he said, "Stay at the BOQ (Bachelor Officers' Quarters) over here." And he said, "It'll just be for a couple of nights and then we'll see what to do with you." He added, "Go there and check in. A clerk will check you in. Store your gear and sleep there." Well, once again there was no air-conditioning, even in the BOQ at that time. It was hot as it could be and humid, but at least in this room there were four giant fans. I quite logically thought, "Well, here's a great big bed, you know, and a clean bathroom to myself and everything." I'm having the time of my life. I turned the fans on, and about two o'clock in the morning there's this hammering on the door. I get up and open the door, and this guy in the hallway says, "What the hell are you doing in my room?" He was a bird colonel, and I was in the VIP quarters. So, I said,

"I'm sorry, sir." I recognized the rank, even at that hour. He said, "Get the hell out of here," so I packed up my bag at two o'clock and was going back over to the adjutant. When I told him I got thrown out of my room, he said, "What the hell? I put you in the wrong quarters." The problem was his at that point, not mine.

One thing that's important to remember about air force service at that time was that we were not far removed from World War II. The B-25s in which we flew were retreads from the war, and a lot of personnel were still around. Guys who were flying the planes—the pilots who were flying the student navigators—many of them were at the end of their careers and sweating it out to get twenty years. In general, they were quite crusty guys, and they had been through it, you know. They had been over there. There were some great guys and some great instructors. When I went to Connally Air Force Base near Waco, I had a roommate who was a pilot. His first name was Ray, but I don't remember his last name. He was six-foot-four with bright red hair, and he had flown fighters. When the canopy came down, he had to duck so it didn't hammer him into the cockpit. Somehow, he had been in Vietnam. I never could understand that; he had been a trainer of some kind in Vietnam in the fifties. At the time I knew him, I had no idea where Vietnam was. I had never heard of it. Apparently, he had been working with the French and was an instructor or a teacher of some kind. A tremendous pilot. He had a dog named Bomber, a German Shepherd, and of course the air force had a rule that there were to be no dogs in the barracks. Well, here comes Bomber, and Bomber and Red and I lived together for about six months. The dog was a great big monster, you know, but a very nice dog, and we tended to party a lot, even though Waco was bone dry.

We had strict instructions to not date any girls from Baylor University, so of course that was like the handbook I mentioned earlier. Truthfully, Baylor officials did not seem to care; it was the air force that was concerned about the situation. If we partied too much the night before a flight, though, we took that into account the next day. If Ray did not feel like he could fly the B-25, he had ways to cover. First of all, he limped a great deal, sort of like John Wayne in *The High and the Mighty*. He would kind of limp around during the inspection and take his time looking at the airplane. Eventually, he would get in the thing and we would taxi out to the end of the runway. I would be on there with a couple of other students and a copilot, and he would call the tower at Connally and say, "We have a mag [magneto] drop on number-two engine. We can't possibly fly this mission." In truth, he was just too hungover to do it. And the guy in the tower one time said, "We'll send you a chief out to look for it." It didn't fall off the plane, of course, so he just said, "We've just got a mag drop on my instrument panel and this plane is unflyable." So, we would taxi it back in. He would go back in with the flight crew, and the crew chief would come up and say, "There's nothing wrong with this plane," and Ray would say, "No, something's wrong with me." With that, he would head to the officers' club, which was wet. There, he would see how much beer he could drink until he felt better. I don't know what in the world ever happened to him, but he was a colorful guy.

As noted in the introduction, the Strategic Air Command predated the US Air Force by one year. When World War II was winding down, they created the Strategic Air Command (SAC) within the US Army Air Forces, and it remained there when the service became the US Air Force. Its mission was to prepare for a global attack. The US command had this opportunity to fly long-range aircraft anywhere in the world, and it became feasible to do so only with the advent of aerial refueling. It had been around for a while and was tried out in Europe on a maneuver called a "probe and drogue." The boom came down from the tanker, and it looked like a firehose with a basketball hoop on the end of it, and that would hook onto the nose of the airplane and transfer fuel. It was considered unusable at first, though, because it had not been fully tested. It was General LeMay who realized its possibility, and he nourished that idea and really built SAC on the concept. There was a philosophy when I became an old and experienced navigator, no longer a cadet, that navigators were the most important people on the plane because they got you there to do your job, and the pilots were the truck drivers. They just drove the thing and the navigator was the guy who, first, got you to your target and then, second, as navigators eventually became bombardiers, too, dropped the weapons. After all that, the pilot then drove you back to your base.

The pilot was in command all the time, except when, on a Norden bombsight operation (like the B-25s utilized), he would, at a crucial point close to the target, say, "Bombardier, you've got the aircraft." At that point, the power to steer that airplane came down to a little lever on the Norden, and you could vary the direction of that airplane by eighteen degrees, thirty-six degrees, and then eighteen degrees off the pure. In visual days, the bombardier would look down and see the target coming and know where it was going to be, and he could then steer that plane. The first time I did that, I thought I had died and gone to heaven. The smallest adjustment made a big difference, and the plane would respond beautifully. A thirty-six-degree span is fairly large, and the controls allowed the bombardier to go back and forth and up and down. On a final bomb run in a B-25, the bombardier would take over at about 250 knots—about 15 minutes prior—if he had a visual on the target. It was highly untechnical. When you saw it, though, the training kicked in. As the bombardier, I had studied the terrain and knew what the target looked like, so I would put the crosshairs of the Norden right on the thing and could calculate the distance to the target and how many degrees I had to vary. It was not a comfortable maneuver, because the bombardier had to bend over the instrument and sometimes use a backward hand move, and of course there was a great deal of tension. However, for a brief time, I was the pilot and I was flying that plane.

Although I enjoyed being a part of SAC, it was considered something to avoid during Air Training Command. It was not the place a lot of airmen wanted to be, primarily because of Curtis Emerson LeMay, who had a reputation of being an officer-eater. If you did not perform, you were gone. SAC was his baby. Although LeMay is most closely associated with SAC, George Kenney had it first. He had been Gen. Douglas MacArthur's air force commander in the Southwest Pacific, which must have driven him nuts. MacArthur had no use for airplanes at all. He wanted to land and attack man-on-man. Kenney, who commanded the Fifth Air Force, nevertheless survived the general to become commander of SAC. He did not really want it, though. He was burned out after a long military career, so it was a reluctant command. What he really wanted to do was to serve as an air advisor for the United Nations. Once the air force command figured this all out, they picked LeMay, an absolute wartime hero who was bloodthirsty and direct, and who accomplished his mission. Nothing else counted. They called him Iron Ass, to his face even. At times, they changed that to Iron Eagle to be polite, but the derivation was Iron Ass because of his command of the Eighth Air Force. Under his direction, it went to the Pacific and oversaw the nuclear weapon advent. He loved it, because here was the answer to his prayer, which was, some argued, to kill everybody—and all he had to do was push a button.

4
From Mole Hole to Airborne

When I was at Ellington and Connally, they were both part of the Air Training Command, headquartered out of Randolph Air Force Base, northeast of San Antonio. All training bases were part of that command. We had heard about the Strategic Air Command, though. Personnel we encountered would tell us stories about how LeMay led, what the crews had to go through, and how terrible it was. But, they would remind us, if you succeeded, you were on the way. Promotions were expedited, and there were other special considerations they used to encourage people to move on up. LeMay's reputation certainly preceded him, and these young guys, second lieutenants, felt like they did not want to do that. So, a week before I got out of Connally, they called together the graduating class (class 5405) in a big room when we received our third rating (1521 rating). At that point, they offered every officer his choice of where he would like to serve—what command and what base. So, the guy in charge said, "Write up what you want and take it to the commanding officer, and it'll be fully considered. We usually give navigators what they want, because it's such a technical thing." Taking him at his word, I wrote down March Air Force Base, in California, Military Air Transport Service (MATS). Essentially, it was an air force airline, and all they did was ferry troops around the world utilizing the big C-124s. They had the loudest brakes, by the way, and it seemed like you could hear the 124s brakes a hundred miles away. I thought March AFB would be ideal. It was next to Los Angeles. I would thus get to the West Coast and really have a big time. I was planning to go on fourteen days of leave and then go to Riverside, California, and report at March. I had just gotten home on my leave, however, and I received a telegram saying, "You've been assigned to Smoky Hill Air Force Base, Salina, Kansas, Strategic Air Command, 40th Bomb Wing." I looked on a map and discovered it was about seventy miles from Wellington, Kansas. I felt a bit like Humphrey Bogart in *Casablanca*. Of all the air bases in the world, why this? Smoky Hill AFB, later renamed Schilling, was a World War II base that became one of the first SAC facilities after the war.

One of the things that always concerned me about my training was that I thought I might not make it because it required a great deal of math, and I simply had difficulties in that regard, as my high school math teacher, Mr. DeVore, well knew. I was dating a girl who was a math instructor at Rice Institute, though, and she would brief me on such things. I mean, she really tried. You know, the air force instructors got into trigonometry and geometry, obviously, with the angle of attack and all this kind of stuff, and I was just lost. My girlfriend would say, "You are the stupidest guy I've ever seen when it comes to math. Can you add?" And I said, "Yeah, I can do that." It was just an absolute challenge for me. Nobody ever believes this, but it is the God's truth: When I got to the final exam to get the first set of wings, the primary wings, I looked over the exam and there were ten multiple choice questions dealing with algebra. I did not know a single answer. I just figured I had nothing to lose, except I could be a supply officer somewhere and get out in two years instead of four. So, I went C, A, B, A, C, A, B, B, A, C. Somehow I got 75 percent and passed. I never used algebra again and was never called upon to utilize it. I know that discomforts some regarding our military, but it is simply the truth. All the work thankfully became computerized, so the computers did the calculations.

Now, this was in 1954 when I began working with computers. The navy invented them, in effect, and the air force picked them up, and it got to the point on the T-29, for example, that when I was radar bombing, I simply cranked in the coordinates we wanted to hit and the airplane would go right to it. I did not have to do anything other than that. I would, though, put in what I thought the wind speed was. The airplane computer could not figure out wind direction, but it maintained a course. I would just enter what the wind was doing—either slowing it down or whatever—so it was not dead reckoning anymore. Dead reckoning, a fascinating form of navigation in use since the time of the Phoenicians, no longer existed. It gave way to the computers. Under the previous system, I would compute a course from point A to point B and draw a line on the map. That was the true course. I then went to the weather office, and the personnel there would give me the wind speed and direction. They might say, for example, the wind is out of the east at fifty miles an hour and is going to blow you off course. I cranked in the magnetic heading, because the compass did not agree with the course line, and I could compute, using the known ground speed, what time we would get to the target. That was just basic navigation with no aids and no electronics. If a navigator was good enough and paid attention, he could learn to read the wind, because that is what drove the calculation of air speed—in effect, the ground speed the plane was making into the wind. It was an enjoyable and satisfying process when it all went right. We got good at figuring wind speed through observation. We would sometimes fly so low that we could tell the direction and the strength of the wind by flags flying on flagpoles. At twenty-five knots, for example, the flag is out straight, and I could tell the direction, obviously, without having too much trouble. So, based on such observations, I might say, OK, the weather guys are wrong, the wind has changed, or a front has come through. It was extremely imprecise and somewhat like flying by the seat of the pants, but I could rely on my visual sense. Coming down out of the clouds, I would spot a flag and make an immediate determination: if that flag is going twenty-five miles an hour and we are heading straight east right into that wind, it is zero-nine-zero, twenty-five degrees. It was basic problem solving, and even though I did not like math, I enjoyed that.

Navigators became more and more important with the advent of nuclear weaponry. We could not make any mistakes. If you could not hit the target, you wiped out whole civilizations. You know, a lot of psychological stuff went into it, along with a lot of briefing. Can you do this? Can you drop a weapon knowing you are going to kill two hundred thousand people with it? There was also, as you might imagine, a lot of debriefing. My approach was always, "Well, here I am. It is my job." The debriefing, though, made sure that I could separate my regular thinking from the mission. Could I lose that killer instinct instilled by SAC? And it took about three days talking to a psychiatrist to ensure normalcy. He would give you that thing about going down the road and seeing a school bus full of kids. Do you turn your car, or do you hit the bus? I guess a SAC-trained killer would say, "Hell, I'd hit the bus. I'm going to survive." You get into the thing, though, and really you could see what they were doing. They were bringing us back to civilian life—depressurizing us, I guess.

The pressure was terrific in SAC because of Curtis LeMay, because of the importance of the mission, and because the future of the country during the Cold War was at stake. You had to avoid messing up at all costs because the stakes were so high. The mission might entail flying inside enemy territory—the enemy being the Soviets at the time—flying right down the coastline. I could see it clearly on the radar. There's the coastline and there is Vladivostok, you know, a big blip on the coast. There were also the interceptors, with Soviet fighters coming up on radar as well. The pressure of that was so terrific, and everybody was just brittle. I have long contended that is one reason the officers' clubs on SAC bases were so popular. SAC encouraged drinking. Martinis, for example, cost ten cents, and there were no limits back then. It was a simple matter of coping or blowing off steam.

Officers' clubs were just jocular places, with people laughing and singing, because it was like, "Phew! I'm back. I didn't get shot down. I didn't fly into a tree." The pressure on SAC bases was so immense, whereas in other commands, maybe in the Tactical Air Command (TAC), you were, in effect, flying your own airplane and were in command of that ship. In SAC, you were a member of a crew, and the aircraft commander made the initial decisions, but from there on it was the navigator's job. Most people, given the right training, could learn to fly an airplane—take off, land, pay attention to the rules, and not crash. The navigator, though, was under much more pressure. The pilot never made a mistake to be demoted or kicked out, but the navigator could miscalculate and put you immediately in harm's way. I had a friend who, when flying to get to England, went up the Irish

Channel, thinking it was the English Channel, and then overflew the Republic of Ireland. He was leading three other planes, so he led all four tankers across Ireland. Of course, their radar picked it up, and the air force had to pay on the weight of the airplane and the number of miles flown over. I thought he was going to get kicked out, but he somehow survived.

Smoky Hill, located at the edge of the agricultural town of Salina, was not a modern base. It had been deactivated at the end of World War II but reactivated in the mid-1950s. My wife, Capy, and I went back there a few years ago, and there is nothing there now. At some juncture, the government came along and tore all the old buildings down. There had been several huge, cavernous, old-fashioned hangars, and the barracks were primitive, of minimal construction, and just really fierce. There was little to do at Smoky Hill in my era but go to the officers' club and drink, and drive sports cars and smoke cigars, mainly because LeMay did the same things.

I was never quite sure why I was selected for SAC. I felt like I had a hard time figuring out the basic stuff and was, therefore, not at the head of my class. I had no real mechanical ability and no mathematical ability, initially, and that combination could have been deadly. At some point, though, the light inexplicably went on and I was suddenly able to grasp everything. Somehow, I compensated for previous shortcomings and got to the point where I was pretty good, and eventually I became an instructor. All along the way, I was being monitored and evaluated with regard to my capabilities and potential, and in the end, out of a class of more than forty, there were four of us selected by SAC.

Although the early 1950s were, in general, a time of fear and mistrust internationally, that did not pervade in the air force. I felt, and justifiably so, this mentality was the determining factor in the concept of mutual destruction. It is my opinion that if SAC had not existed, and if LeMay had not been so notably belligerent, I think the Soviets would have come over and blown the place to pieces, because they had the capability, including nuclear arsenals, to do it. But it was like, if you kill us, we are going to kill you, in whatever sequence it is going to take, and at the end of it there will be nothing left of anybody. Of course, the Soviets had the nuclear capability even sooner than we thought. That was often the case with other technologies. We guarded the Norden bombsights with our lives, for example, and we actually swore an oath that we would die defending that piece of equipment. Later on in World War II, though, we found out the Germans had similar technology.

Prior to the Norden bombsight, everything was visual. You see the target; you release the bomb. In the days of the open cockpits, the bombs were literally thrown overboard and subjected to natural forces on their way down. Although the early bombs, including the ones I worked with, had no flight capabilities, they had a trajectory that moved forward some from when it was dropped, given inertia, but they eventually went straight down. With the dropping of the atomic bomb from the Enola Gay, the crew had no idea how far that thing was going to blow. From even miles away, they felt the jolt when it went off. Of course, that was an atomic bomb, and the hydrogen bombs were fifty times as powerful. Films from that area indicate they dropped the weapon and then kind of just hoisted the aircraft right straight up. You can see the plane's pitching. The crews still felt the jolt when it went off, even though they were a long way from it. But that was a huge explosion, and that was just atomic; you get into the hydrogen bomb, and that made like fifty atomics.

Our work with bombs came along after we were elevated to the advanced program. In that, we learned how to aim bombs, how to arm them and disarm them, and how to fly with them to understand the weight dynamics and other aspects. When I started flying aboard B-25s, we used eighty-pound practice bombs. We used to bomb Mustang Island at Port Aransas along the Texas coast, where my family now goes for vacations, and I often have this premonition that I will step on a live one and detonate it and myself. The practice bombs, though, were loaded with flour, so that when they hit the ground the flour would puff out and you could measure your accuracy. In SAC, though, we got radar evaluation readings via ground stations. We would be in contact with the ground as we were approaching, for example, the railroad marshalling yards in Fort Worth. On approaching the target, we would contact the ground station, which would let us know if we were on target, and then we would drop this mythical bomb on the railyards. The system would then print up the results.

If we got within a quarter mile, that passed; outside of that, though, it was a busted mission and we had to go again. Circular error (CE) drove navigators and crews crazy, but that was really how they got evaluated. That is what it was all about—dropping bombs and having them hit the intended target.

So many questions remain about the effectiveness of bombing programs, even in World War II. I have been in big arguments, usually with navy guys, about the waste of armaments. Some never hit their targets, but those that did only caused brief disruptions. The enemy would quickly rebuild. The situation was exacerbated in Vietnam, where many of the facilities were underground.

After about a year at Smoky Hill, I was combat ready, which meant my training unit, T-36, was finally prepared to go on full military action. Our work had been approved by what were called standboard officers (standardization officers), who flew on every plane on every mission. They would sit next to the navigator's station and grade everything I did. They would help simulate combat conditions, calling for evasive action and other maneuvers. We did not use flight simulators, although there were atmospheric compression chambers for training with oxygen. In those chambers, we had to prove to ourselves how much oxygen we needed over ten thousand feet. At eleven thousand feet simulated altitude, we were required to remove our masks, and in about a minute, air intake seemed critical. We would thus signal to the standboard officer, who would slap the mask back on us, and then we were OK.

Being combat ready was a big deal. It meant that if the ball dropped, as they said, the Klaxon whistle sounded, and within minutes we would be off to someplace to refuel a whole bunch of B-47s, for example. We were on duty twenty-four hours a day, seven days a week, unless we were on leave. If we were in our mole holes—more on that later—we had about seven minutes to get dressed, get out on the field, and get the plane airborne, which was a great challenge. From bed to air in seven minutes—we were timed on that. The mole holes were right on the edge of the active runways, so we just popped up like gophers, hopped in the planes, and were gone.

The mole holes were interesting features of SAC bases. My first book about World War II airfields in Texas, *The Stars Were Big and*

Bright, included a chapter on Amarillo Army Airfield.¹ A nice gentleman at the museum up there called and said, "I know a guy you should meet. He's the fire marshal for Amarillo International Airport, and he knows everything about when it was part of SAC." So, I went out there, and the guy said, "Boy, I'm glad to talk to you. Let me show you something. I have keys to the mole hole." So, we went down in that thing, and it was like a movie set or like stepping onto a base where everyone had died. There was still toilet paper on the roll and sheets on the bed, but all the personnel were gone.

On a normal day, we were in the mole holes and prepared for action. Inside them would be about four crews. A tanker crew consisted of six airmen—the aircraft commander, pilot, engineer, navigator, boom operator, and radio operator—but there were others hanging around, like the standboard guys. When the Klaxon went off—and it was a godforsaken alarm that scared us near to death—the ground crew came and opened the big bay doors for us, and we just came running out of there. Depending on what airplane we were scheduled to fly, if it was too far away to run to get to it in seven minutes, they had pickups sitting there, warmed up, ready to go. We would jump in the back of the pickups, carrying our parachutes, and off we went to the plane and takeoff. The planes were all prechecked. The preflight ground checks had all been done. Usually, the pilot was responsible for that, but the crew chiefs took over that task on the alert airplanes. By the time we got there, the engines were turning, so we just hopped up in there and took off. We had direct clearance. Anybody else in the air anywhere within a hundred miles of it was cleared. So here came SAC. The B-47s would go off first, followed by the tankers. I guess probably eight to ten bombers would go first, which was an amazing thing to see. If you were near the runway, the roar literally shook the ground. After the bombers were airborne, the tankers followed suit. The noise from both the jets and conventional aircraft was truly deafening.

No planes circled the field. Once airborne, we went directly to the target. It was always to the north at that time, because we were prepared to fight the Soviets. They would have come over the North Pole, so we were on a polar route from the other way. Once we got to the pole, the compasses began to spin out of control, so we got no direction from them. Below, we could see nothing—just a vast white blanket of nothingness. The flights were both fascinating and rewarding. For me, to navigate a long-range mission and come in within a minute of our ETA (estimated time of arrival) and right on target—that was everything. On a long-range mission, we might go from Kansas to Greenland, which was incredible. Or we might go from Smoky Hill to Goose Bay, Labrador, and then from Goose Bay to England to cross the Atlantic. In those days there were weather ships that sat out in the middle of the Atlantic Ocean, and my favorite was Radio Ship *November*. Why it had that name, I do not know, but we would get within two hundred miles of Radio Ship *November* and call it. They would say, "We've got you, Air Force 771, on track. Your ETA is exactly right. Maintain your current heading and you'll hit the English coast." We were not halfway there, but we were on course. Once we got off the British coast, English radar would pick us up and talk us on in. That is, unless, of course, like the navigator I mentioned earlier, you made a mistake in your calculations.

5
Fallout over Falun

Within the context of the midair refueling process, the boom operator had one of the hairiest jobs in the SAC. When we were refueling an aircraft like the B-47, there were thirteen feet between us and the bomber. The tanker was going as fast as it could go and literally redlined. The four engines were just going bam, bam, bam, and we were making 285 knots maybe. The B-47, on the other hand, was as slow as it could go and was wallowing back and forth. At times, since I had little to do during the refueling, I would walk around and observe the operation. I could see the B-47's aircraft commander's face clearly from fourteen feet away, and often they would wave at me while the fuel was going right in the nose of the bomber. The hose went down and had a magnetic connector on it that made a loud mechanical clicking sound when it connected. At that point, we started offloading the fuel. As it transferred, the bomber was getting heavier and we were getting lighter, so the tanker starts going up. Offloading 240,000 pounds of fuel made a dramatic weight differential in the air. The tanker flew smoother, but the bomber then had to adjust, and in doing so looked something like a hummingbird in flight at a pronounced nose-up angle. It took very good pilots to keep planes from stalling out. From my vantage point, it looked precarious, with the bomber wings wobbling. Had it stalled, of course, it would have torn the boom off, and in fact, that happened from time to time. The stress on the plane and crew was phenomenal. I could almost hear rivets popping. The plane was vibrating wildly, and the engineer was no doubt sweating, but the fuel kept moving. If we were lucky and had no weather problems, we could offload the 240,000 pounds of fuel in about 15 minutes. For those who want to get a feeling for the operation, I recommend the refueling scene in the movie *Strategic Air Command*.[1] While the depiction is the most realistic I have seen on film, it does take place against the backdrop of Mount Rainier, with glorified music in the background. That part, of course, I don't remember.

There were occasions where everything did not go as planned and we would have to wave someone off because of dangerous complications. I remember we were in England twice on temporary duty and were refueling fighters. We were flying over a racetrack course between Norwich and Ipswich, and this Air National Guard pilot out of the Midwest—Ohio or Iowa—hooked his fighter onto our tanker. We could refuel about four fighters, because they took less fuel than bombers. In the refueling process, this young pilot, for reasons unknown, decided he had had enough and just broke off and took the boom with him. For a longtime afterward, I kept a newspaper clipping related to the incident. The article told of potato workers on a farm down below who reported that pieces of stovepipe fell out of the sky, but they never knew the source. Well, it was us who dropped that "stovepipe." When the incident occurred, I had been lying alongside the boom operator, who was on his belly, flying the apparatus. All of a sudden there was this loud sound—wham!—and the guy just goes off. You are supposed to say, "Break away, break away, break away." He said nothing, though; he just went. He broke away without telling anybody. We had enough boom hanging out of that plane that it would hit the ground if we were to land. There was no way to bring it up, because he took the cables with him. We were half full of fuel and thus highly volatile at landing. Our aircraft commander said, "Shut everything off: radios, radar, the whole bit. The slightest spark and that thing will go, and we'll go with it." There were thousands of pounds of highly flammable av (aviation) gas still in there—highly volatile, flammable stuff. It was not far to our base at Brize Norton, so we flew back. As we approached, the pilot broke the radio silence and said, "Emergency declared." Workers immediately foamed the runway, and the plane landed and just sort of waltzed down on that foam. The pilot was trying so hard to keep the nose of the plane high so the boom would not drag, because a spark could come all the way up and ignite that gas, and that would have been the end of us right there. But he kept it up while the boom slid down that foam, and finally the plane just kind of did a little do-si-do—kind of turned around suddenly and stopped. We were on a huge runway, a WWII-variety B-17 runway, and the plane came to a halt about fifty feet from the RAF station officers' club. All these guys were out watching it. Everybody knew this was going on, so they all came out to watch the action—all the fire trucks and ambulances and other equipment. We all jumped out of the plane, fearing it might blow at any time. I looked up and there was my friend Walter Sherman at the club. He was smoking a cigarette and gestured for me to come on over.

What is interesting about the refueling process back then was it relied to an extent on the law of averages. A B-47 took off basically with just enough fuel to lift off, get to altitude, and get to the target or rendezvous point. That depended on the mission, but they could reach a good range with the initial fuel. When the tankers were there waiting for them at the rendezvous point, though, then they could really complete their mission, and that was the function. They traveled in pods, three B-47s at a time, and we would refuel all three of them. If we had any fuel left over, we would just stay up there and orbit around some beautiful and isolated parts of the world. When our own fuel got low, though, we would head home. We could not be refueled in flight, obviously, so we would go back and sit around for a couple of days and then get called into the mole hole again, and off we would go.

The biggest fear I ever had on refueling runs was not finding the receiver, because any delays increased the tension. When the B-47 came within range of the specified rendezvous, there was an IFF (identify friend or foe) receiver that would send out a signal. It is hard to explain, but it was like little bars—almost like an early barcode, I guess—and a transmitter in the B-47 would send this out, and the little bars on the radar would be like one and three little bars, and then maybe two. It changed by aircraft. And the navigator has got his radar going and he's on the course; the navigator on the B-47 then gets the signal when within range of that tanker. It was always rewarding to see those blips begin to appear. At that point, the navigator took over and talked the bomber pilot up to the boom. On site verification, the boom operator took over and would say, "OK, sir, you are five miles and closing. I've got you in sight and the boom's coming down."

During the Cold War, the flight crews at times presented an interesting mix of experience and age. The aircraft commander was probably in his early thirties. I had an engineer who was a World War II retread, out of the hills somewhere—the crudest human being you ever wanted to meet. He was a slob, and nobody could stand him, but he was a good engineer. We had a squadron navigator, a lead navigator, who had also been in World War II. By the time of the Cold War, he was probably in his late thirties or early forties. For the most part, the navigators were all relatively young. A B-47 crew was a bit older, because they had taken more training. It would take them longer to get there than it did us, I guess, but I would say probably a median age of thirty. They say in World War II there were guys flying B-29s who were not old enough to get a driver's license.

While some crew members had to deal with airsickness, especially when refueling planes were bouncing around quite a bit, I was lucky and avoided that malady. In my instructor days we would fly long missions, like from San Francisco to Hawaii or Wake Island, and I would use the dead time to get some sleep. Station 230 was the bulkhead. It was right behind the navigator's station—this hard, metal floor of an airplane. We had these great big parkas in case we went down, so I would make a bed out of a parka and go to sleep—no restraint, no safety belt, nothing. The plane might be rocking and yawing, but I would just sleep like a baby.

Parachuting, however, is something else. It was a great experience, although I would not recommend it for most people. I am not sure why anybody does it on purpose. I parachuted once on a mission, but not intentionally. Parachute training started at Ellington Field. They had a technique called the PLF—parachute landing fall—where we jumped off a platform into a sawdust pit. There was a certain way we were supposed to land, but I do not believe I ever did it the right way. It was a sort of hit and roll action. We would land on one foot and then kind of roll over and get up without any problem. My favorite parachute story took place at Ellington, although I will save the story of my only jump for later. In this particular case, we were all lined up for preflight inspection with the aircraft commander in a training squadron, walking up and down, and the parachutes were the chest packs. They had a big harness we wore all the time, and we just hooked the pack on that. We did not wear the packs during inspection, though. We were standing there getting briefed on the mission when word came out that a hurricane was on its way to Houston. It had been predicted, and sure enough here it came. The commander said, "OK, grab your 'chutes; we're going back into Operations." Well, I picked mine up by the D-ring that pulled the ripcord, so the parachute popped out. I was standing there holding this metal thing with a chain hanging off it, and the parachute's blowing down the runway. The guy who was the commander said, "Oh, for God's sake." He looked around with absolute, total disgust.

I must admit that all the parachute training had no effect on me at all, because at the time we were supposed to wait to count to ten before pulling the ripcord, so we would clear the vertical tail and the horizontal tail assembly, and not hang up on it. We did not want to do that, either, especially if the plane was going down, because we would be dangling back there. So on that one occasion when I jumped (which I will elaborate on later), I just jumped out and pulled it. We were at fifteen hundred feet, and there it came. I had no regard for the training; I wanted to get the hell out of there. I was convinced we were on fire.

The incident where I had to bail out of the plane occurred on September 5, 1955. My AC (aircraft commander) was an affable sort of guy who had recently received a spot promotion to lieutenant colonel. Spot promotions were Curtis LeMay's pet project. If an officer on a crew really performed well and exceeded expectations, which were quite high, then that crew received a spot promotion, just like a brevet, and moved up a rank and received commensurate pay. We were out on a mission with this particular AC and were coming back to land at Smoky Hill, Kansas. We were flying over Falun, Kansas,[2] at the time and probably at about six or seven thousand feet, and it was around three o'clock in the afternoon. The commander said, "We have a fire on the number-three engine." And the engineer replied, "No we don't, sir. There's no fire out there." "Yes, we do," the AC said. "Fire on the number-three engine. Keep your eye on it." Keep in mind, the AC is the aircraft commander and therefore the absolute commander. When the AC said we had a fire on the number-three engine, you had to believe there was a fire on the number-three engine. The Boeing aircraft were highly reliable airplanes with warning light systems, but there was always the human factor to take into account. He said, "Got a fire warning light on three." "No, sir," said the engineer. "Yes, you do," the AC said once again. Finally, the engineer said, "All right, sir." "Keep your eye on it." "Yes, sir." And the AC said, "That's getting pretty bad. We're going to have to jump." And I thought, because SAC was ridiculous in its drills, *Oh, this is just a game. We're not going to jump out of this airplane.* Regardless, the procedure was that when the plane's emergency bell rang three times, we were to get ready to bail out. One sustained ring and out we went in descending order. Enlisted men went first, and the aircraft commander went last. So, we were sitting there, and he is insisting we have this onboard fire. I'm sitting close to the engineer, who looks at me and says, "What's going on? What is this?" "It's SAC," I replied. I was sure it was a drill. Pretty soon, though, there were three rings—get ready to bail out. We left our stations and, while the plane is descending, everyone lined up—radio operator first, boom operator, engineer, navigator, copilot, and aircraft commander. When the sustained ring sounded, the boom operator opened the rear hatch and out we went with nothing between us and the ground except a nylon canopy strapped to our bodies. The radio operator stood in the open hatch until somebody pushed him out. Down he went, flailing wildly, and quickly everybody jumped out in order, including the copilot, leaving only the lieutenant colonel on there, flying the plane. Meanwhile, we drifted on down and it was almost ethereal. I felt like I was in a dream.

    Regardless, I was monkeying around with the shroud lines, trying to direct my course. There was a great big depression in the ground outside the little town, and it looked like a dry lake or something. I remember thinking, *Better to land there than in a tree.* I kept aiming my parachute toward this feature, but it turned out it was not dry—it was a lake that had mud. So, I landed in the mud, which aside from the dirt and grime probably couldn't be a better place to land. The parachute collapsed, so I was not dragged through the muck, but the whole right side of my flight suit, boot and everything, got covered in it. I watched the copilot hit the ground. I waited for him, and together we walked the short distance to the tiny town of Falun, where the only business was a small country store. It was regulation to pick up your parachute, so we trudged along, dragging those silly 'chutes. There were three guys sitting on the porch, just like something out of a sitcom. They were rocking away, smoking their pipes. They had obviously seen us coming down, and here come these two guys in flight suits dragging their parachutes. I remember asking one of the pipe smokers, "How you doing?" "OK." I'm looking around through the puff of smoke coming up, and I ask, "You guys have a telephone in the store?" He said, "Yes sir, there sure is." "Could I use it for a quick call to the air base?" "Yes, I suppose so," he replied. I said, "Charge for it?" "No, no charge." I went in to call Smoky Hill, and I told Operations what had happened and where we were. Operations said, "OK, we'll send a truck out to pick you up. It'll be about thirty, forty-five minutes before we can get there." So, we're sitting there, and I always carried a dollar bill in my flight suit—never anything else. They had a big sign that said, "Schlitz Beer." I thought, *Oh, man, that would taste pretty good after falling out of that airplane.* I said, "You guys sell beer?" "Yeah, we do." "I've got a dollar here. Can I get a couple of cans of beer?" They said, "Well, tell you what. On the house." So, we drank that beer, and I saved my dollar and put it back in the flight suit. About this time the truck came and picked us up and took us back to Smoky Hill. When we got there, we learned the aircraft commander had landed our plane by himself and that no fire had existed after all.

SAC was really upset about the incident, because the AC risked the lives of five personnel. They formed a flight evaluation board, which is the kiss of death; it's right next to court martial. As crew members, eyewitnesses, and participants in this ridiculous event, we were called upon to testify, and our stories were right down the line and never varied. I never heard the AC testify, though, because he went in for a one-on-one deposition. It came down to the final day to decide what was going to happen to him, and the hearing room door opened and in walked Curtis Emerson LeMay. As soon as he entered, we all snapped to attention without being told to. There was no question about who it was. You could hear one man saying, "God, it's LeMay." He was about five-foot-ten, I guess, and smoking a pipe on that occasion. He was a burly guy who just exuded power—one of the most powerful looking guys I ever saw. He walked over with the base commander and sat down. The investigating officer repeated what had happened. LeMay then looked at the convening board that was to determine our aircraft commander's future. They all looked at him and he was shaking his head no, and that was it. That erring pilot was finished at that point. He lost his aeronautical rating and promotion, went back two ranks to captain, and received a reassignment as a supply officer somewhere. He was gone instantly, and I never spoke with him. LeMay, though, just got up and walked out. We all came to attention again, and he got back on his plane and off he went—flew it himself, of course. I think if LeMay had not come, the guy might have gotten away with it, but it was obviously a breach of protocol, to say the least. I was never sure what had caused the incident. The pilot swore he had seen a warning light, but Boeing officials and representatives of the Inspector General and the USAF checked the plane thoroughly and found no evidence of a fire. As a result, they cleared the plane for flight, and we continued our work as the crew with a new aircraft commander.

The author at an air show in Greenville, Texas, circa 1999. (Courtesy of the author's collection.)

The author at the Strategic Air Command Museum, Omaha, Nebraska, circa 2001. (Courtesy of the author's collection.)

Capt. Tom Alexander, instructor-navigator, Illinois Air National Guard, circa 1968. (Courtesy of the author's collection.)

Tom Alexander (*second from left, front row*) with his KC-97 flight crew at Brize Norton Royal Air Force Station, England, 1955. (Courtesy of the author's collection.)

Tom Alexander (*left*) with his buddy Walt Sherman at Sidi Slimane Air Base, French Morocco, 1955. (Courtesy of the author's collection.)

SAC war room, date unknown. (Courtesy of Ben Guttery, Collections Manager, Fort Worth Aviation Museum, Texas; Frank Kleinwechter Collection, B-36 Peacemaker Museum, via Don Pyeatt.)

"Aerial view of SAC command, post construction, looking west." Offutt Air Force Base, Nebraska, Strategic Air Command Headquarters and Command Center. (Library of Congress Prints and Photographs, HAER NE-9-M-63.)

"SAC command center, main operations area, underground structure, building 501, undated." Offutt Air Force Base, Nebraska. (Library of Congress Prints and Photographs, HAER NE-9-N-9.)

"A model of Strategic Air Command's latest heavy bomber, the B-52, is discussed by General Curtis E. LeMay, SAC Commander (*left*) and Field Marshall Viscount Montgomery, Deputy Supreme Allied Commander in Europe, during the latter's visit to Headquarters Strategic Air Command (November 1954). During his staff at Offutt Air Force Base, Neb., he was briefed on the world-wide operations and capabilities of SAC." (Library of Congress Prints and Photographs, Unprocessed in PR 13 CN 1977:072.)

Air force photograph of Gen. Curtis LeMay, taken after 1951, when he became a four-star general. (Wikimedia Commons.)

The Convair T-29 Flying Classroom, US Air Force navigation trainer, in flight. (Courtesy of Ben Guttery, Collections Manager, Fort Worth Aviation Museum, Texas; Convair publicity photo by Don Pyeatt.)

Strategic Air Command shield adopted by the US Air Force in 1952. (Courtesy of Ben Guttery, Collections Manager, Fort Worth Aviation Museum, Texas; Frank Kleinwechter Collection, B-36 Peacemaker Museum, via Don Pyeatt.)

Vintage aircraft flew over the Texas Capitol on September 2, 2015, as part of the Texas World War II initiative, led by Commissioner Thomas E. Alexander of the Texas Historical Commission. (Courtesy of the Texas Historical Commission.)

World War II–era postcard of Smoky Hill Army Air Field, Salina, Kansas. (U.S. Army Air Forces, USGOV-PD.)

Editor Dan K. Utley and author Thomas E. Alexander at a presentation on their book, *Faded Glory*, 2013. (Courtesy of the Texas Historical Commission.)

Aerial view of a KC-97 (*right*) offloading fuel to a B-47 (*left*), 1950s. (Courtesy of Ben Guttery, Collections Manager, Fort Worth Aviation Museum, Texas; National Archives and Records Administration, Record Group 342-B, via Don Pyeatt and Dennis Jenkins.)

View of the refueling operation from the viewpoint of the KC-97 crew. Note the face of the B-47 pilot. (Courtesy of Ben Guttery, Collections Manager, Fort Worth Aviation Museum, Texas; National Archives and Records Administration, Record Group 342-B, via Don Pyeatt and Dennis Jenkins.)

The same refueling operation, this time from the viewpoint of the B-47 pilot looking up to the KC-97 and the boom. (Courtesy of Ben Guttery, Collections Manager, Fort Worth Aviation Museum, Texas; National Archives and Records Administration, Record Group 342-B, via Don Pyeatt and Dennis Jenkins.)

6

A Stream and a Swagger

Wandering off the airfield a bit, I need to clarify a couple of key aspects of my reminiscences. At no point during any of this do I want to indicate that I was any kind of a hero. I was just one of the troops. I never did anything spectacular at all, except that I did my duty that I had to do and needed to do. Nobody shot at me, at least. The second thing to note is that there is a stream of alcohol that runs through these military memories. I need to clarify that I am not an alcoholic. In fact, I have not had a drink of hard liquor since 1972. When I swore off, I swore off, and that was the end of it. I think it was the fuel of the air force for a while, though, because it took the pressure off. Alcohol had its place, to be sure, starting with the seemingly innocent tradition of the mission-ending "tot." When we would land back at Operations, the flight personnel would go off for a visit with the debriefing officer. During the routine flights in the states, the questions were standard: Did anything happen? Was everything OK? Were there any incidents we should know about? Did the radar malfunction? Was there any reason why you thought the mission was not going to work? It was just an informal, one-on-one discussion. In England, though, flying over there with NATO, the English (i.e., the Royal Air Force, RAF) made use of a tradition borrowed from the Royal Navy. Upon landing, each crew member got a little tot, perhaps a half a jigger, of rum. A crew member would take that little rum with him and go into the debriefing, and over there the debriefings were far more intensive. The crewman, who might have been up for twelve hours and under quite a bit of pressure, would knock back that little tot of rum while talking to the officer. It is not a stimulant, as most might think; it was just the reverse. It was a depressant, but it still could bring a tired crewman back to life. In an effort to make the most of the tradition, my friend Walter Sherman and I identified everybody in the entire squad who was a teetotaler. We would approach them after the debriefing and say, "Are you going to drink your rum?" "No, I'm not. Do you want it?" "OK, thanks."

This guy Walter Sherman was an interesting fellow. He looked like Paul Newman, stood about six-foot-three, and was very athletic and extremely attractive to the opposite sex. Everybody liked him. He had that charming personality. He was from Colorado, and we belonged to the same fraternity, Sigma Alpha Epsilon. He had gone to Colorado State University and I had gone to the University of Colorado, and we graduated the same year and went into nav (navigation) training in the US Air Force. He was in Harlingen, in South Texas, and I was at Ellington in Houston. We met when we were assigned to the 40th Bombardment Wing in Smoky Hill Air Force Base, Salina, Kansas, almost simultaneously. He got there about a week before I did.

Walter had a great imagination that did not react well to authority. Having the kind of personality he did, it is perhaps understandable. He did not really have to toe the mark. He had been captain of the Denver championship football team in high school and played football for Colorado State. He married a woman who was a Rhodes Scholar and captain of the rifle team, which I thought was an interesting combination. Anyway, we sort of came together at the same time and were going through the efforts to become combat ready out of the training function, so we could do something genuine. He was a very quick study and became a lead navigator. Once, however, he led a cell of two other tankers on one of our missions to England, and he made a slight navigational error and mistook the St. George Channel for the English Channel. When he realized his mistake, he turned abruptly and took this whole flight of KC-97s across a piece of the Republic of Ireland. At that time, they had all sorts of trouble and consequently scrambled aircraft to come up and see who had penetrated their air space. I was not in that cell. Instead, I went up to the English Channel—the right channel. At the end of the incident, because of his mistake, the air force had to pay weight and distance charge to the Republic of Ireland for each of those planes. It was a sizeable amount of money, but the air force paid it.

As part of the incident, Walter had started his usual descent into Brize Norton, which was outside of Oxford in the central part of England, but his ETA (estimated time of arrival) had to be several hours off. He endured a lot of ribbing about that for the rest of his life, or at least through his duration in the air force. He eventually got tired of being a navigator, after I had gotten out, and he decided to become a pilot. His application was accepted, and the air force sent him down to Hondo Air Force Base, west of San Antonio, for training. He was there for the first part of his flight training but washed out because, of all things, he had a fear of flying. I do not know how many hours he had flying in the plane, but he was just unable to become a pilot. That fear was deeply buried within him, but he was not aware of it until he tried to follow his desire to be a pilot. Nevertheless, he stayed in the air force for a while and became an aide to a major general. The general was commander of some air force unit in the Mediterranean area. Walter rose in rank quickly and was a captain long before I was. I saw him once when he came through Chicago, and he had the fourragère, the big braids on his shoulder, and a chest full of ribbons; he was a crowd stopper.

To be fair and completely honest, I was, early on, frequently guilty of navigational errors in mathematics, but for some reason I would make a compensating error. If I wrote down the correct fifty degrees to the right, somewhere along the way it cancelled itself out. I never missed any entry zones or times or anything. It is important to note, though, the state of relatively primitive navigational equipment at the time. When we entered English airspace, it was ground control radar that guided us to our destination. Traffic over London and England, even forty years ago, was just immense. There was this tiny little island, and SAC had eight bases there in support of the main Soviet Russia containment program, so it was especially busy, in addition to commercial flights coming in all the time.

At Brize Norton, we were assigned to a huge old RAF station. I felt terrific about it, because I loved World War II and all the RAF and Spitfire stories. We were assigned to an open-bay hut out back of the main building, and it had a latrine at one end and about ten bunks. The RAF had used it during the war. They had barely touched it, though, and it was pretty much still just a raw piece of history to me. This was in 1954, so the war had only been over for about ten years. In London, around St. Paul's Cathedral, for example, we could still see just open space and walls where tenements had been, and only basements remained. Some of the shelters were still intact. It really had not changed much, so the cultural landscape was, in effect, a relic of war.

Walter and I, and a few other guys, were in that hut at Brize Norton. By the time our ninety-day duty was over, we were the only two left. We had driven the others off with the parties and so forth. It was an unofficial officers' club, and the people who wanted to have a good time would come in there, but no ranking officers, ever. The highest rank was probably a first lieutenant. One memorable morning we had been up all night flying and had gone to Iceland to buy gin. The air force was running a shuttle service from England to Iceland, where we could get imperial quarts, which were slightly less than forty ounces and duty-free. We would bring the booze back and restock our larder. On one morning in particular, it was about nine o'clock and we were drinking gin while still wearing flight clothes. The door opened and a voice says, "Ten-hut!" Both of us tried to get up, and here was a major general standing in the doorway ready for an inspection. As he walked in, there were glass shards on the floor from people throwing their drinks, and we just heard crunch, crunch, crunch. When he got to where we were standing at attention, he said, "Oh, for God's sake," or something like that, and turned around and walked out. We never heard a word from him after that. He had this tight little grin on his face that said, "I'm not going to touch this." We sat down, and I said, "Yeah, that was a pretty good experience. Don't see many major generals in here."

From Brize Norton, we were eventually dispatched to Sidi Slimane Air Base, one of several stations operated by SAC in what was then French Morocco.[1] We had a hut there as well, but we were a little better behaved at that point. We went into town one night, though, and were advised to be very careful, because even then there were people who loathed the military, particularly US military personnel. Regardless, after a few rounds of champagne, we bought a camel.

It was an old doddering beast, but it came with a rope and a halter. After the purchase, we tied it up outside the place where we were drinking. We sat there and continued drinking, all the time keeping an eye on our camel, who had no idea where he was or who had bought him, and likely did not care. Once we finished, we walked back to the base at the edge of town leading this camel, and the air police guard said, "You can't bring that beast in here." We replied, "Why the hell not? It's tame and is not going to hurt anybody." The guard said, "No, the vet's got to inspect it, so leave it out here." So, we tied the camel to a pole next to the security gate and went out the next morning to check on it, but it was gone. We never saw it again, but we did get written up for that incident. One of our neighbors back at Smoky Hill was a nice guy named Joseph John O'Leary, who unfortunately lived between my place and Walter's. We often cut through his backyard, and I would occasionally play my bugle en route, quite frequently in the early morning hours. O'Leary had tremendous patience, probably because we never took a camel through his yard with us.

As regular pub patrons in England, we fancied ourselves as proficient in the British game of darts. The trouble was that drinking and darts were a problematic combination, especially when the route to the men's room transected with the flight of the projectiles. Even with great precaution, there were near misses. We finally got thrown out of there for causing trouble. Again, it sounds like we were just feckless youth, and I guess we were, but the tension and the pressure of it had to come out somewhere—otherwise we would have gone insane. We could have just sat around thinking of the next flight of seven or eight hours, the consequences of not performing properly, the possibilities of losing an aircraft, running out of fuel, and other dire thoughts. It was serious business while we were at it, but when we were not at it, it was relatively serious nonbusiness, and we pursued that with the same diligence. Being in Great Britain at that time was a memorable experience for me, a future military historian. Evidence of World War II was everywhere. They still had pictures of George VI on the walls and were very much in that frame of royalty, and it really was a wonderful place to be for a great esprit de corps among the officers and parties like that.

Brize Norton was only one of several SAC bases in England at the time, but there were no British troops stationed with us. SAC made them move away and just took over the sites through an agreement with the government. On our R&Rs (rest and relaxation), it was not uncommon for us to travel to Germany. The KC-97 tankers we were flying then would hold a lot of troops in the back, and we would just head out over the channel to places like Munich. I never went to Berlin, although I flew over it, and it looked like a Hollywood set for some apocalyptic movie. Munich was almost that bad. We had just bombed everything in the course of the war. The local people were surprisingly accommodating, however. I think most were so destitute and broke that they would tolerate those of us who were throwing money around like crazy. We used scrip, government-issue bills that served as legal tender in the country wherever we were, and we had stacks of them in various denominations, and we just spread the wealth: twenty-five dollars, ten dollars, whatever. It made a tremendous difference to those people, many of whom had been Nazi troopers only a few years before. I never felt any danger at all. I felt more danger in Morocco. Down there, the Moroccans were just at the beginning of their liberation, and we could feel the tension in the people we encountered there. When we went to Sidi Slimane, we were assigned what we called a batman. Sounds like a cartoon, but our batman was, in effect, our aide, and they had been used by the RAF and the French Air Force alike. When we checked into the barracks, this guy, this batman, came along to assist us. A Muslim who prayed to Mecca five times a day, he did everything for us. He made the beds, cleaned the latrines, and swept the floor, and I do not believe he spoke a word of English. He always had a big smile on his face, but his eyes were just as dead as cesspools. We could tell he thought something was wrong with the arrangement and that he was likely seething inside. Interesting experience. We shared the base with the French Air Force, which probably caused some of the suspected ill will. It could have also stemmed from what might be called the LeMay swagger.

As previously noted, Curtis LeMay was the overriding presence and commanding spirit of SAC. He basically constructed the command out of his own image when he followed George Kenney. When LeMay first took command, he staged mock air raids over big cities just to test the aircraft. Every one of them failed. Not a single one passed on the initial effort, and that convinced him that he had to remake the command with no margin for error. One of his favorite sayings was, "To err is human; to forgive is not SAC policy." He adhered to that letter, because he would fire his best friend if he failed to perform. There was an esprit de corps in that command, however, that is difficult to describe today. Maybe the Navy SEALS and Army Special Ops have it, but SAC had it as well. Essentially, it meant you answered to the highest possible standard of service. No one looked the other way when you were not. It was literally LeMay's way or the highway. We all tried to emulate him. He drove Austin-Healeys and we all, when we could, drove Austin-Healeys. He raced little cars, and we tried to go to races. He smoked cigars all the time, and we all smoked cigars—even in the air. At some points, the cabins would be so full of smoke we could barely see our fellow crew members or the instruments.

It is interesting that LeMay came up through the ROTC program. He was not a West Pointer, one of the few generals who had not trained at the academy, yet he served longer as a general than any other officer in the history of the US Army. He moved through the ranks rapidly, and his performance in World War II was just bloodthirsty. To me, he was an heir to Ulysses S. Grant's military philosophy of total war. People often noted, although not to his face, that he had no regard for innocent citizens. To him, there were no innocent citizens. If they supported the enemy, they were the enemy. He would say, "Fried 'em, roasted 'em, toasted 'em," and brag about it. No one seemed to have him in check. Certainly, Pres. Dwight Eisenhower, earlier his military contemporary, seemed reluctant to reign him in. LeMay could influence Eisenhower and get him to persuade the Senate to give him increasing amounts of money for increasing numbers of airplanes—more and more money to buy more and more airplanes. As a result, SAC became an overwhelming force designed to counter the Soviets, who were of course building up to counter the US effort.

7

The Truth Was in the Stars

The mission was everything to General LeMay. He was not so worried about personal habits and quirks as he was about whether the airmen were able to do what he wanted them to do at the time he wanted them to do it. In that regard, SAC was highly disciplined. The operation flew every day, every morning. Beginning with the briefing, there was no nonsense from then on. There was no horseplay in the air, and there was no conversation going on. We were just dedicated to do our job and to get the airplane where it had to be and get it back, from a navigator point of view. This was before GPS, of course, so with the advent of the new technologies now there are no more navigators – and no more bombardiers, either. As a navigator, I served during a niche in aviation history. It was an interesting niche, however, utilizing an ancient craft that reached back to the Phoenicians. It was an age-honored, time-honored tradition and an art that is simply gone now. (By that, I mean celestial navigation.)

The truth was in the stars. By reckoning with them, we could travel anywhere in the world. With celestial navigation we could keep the airplane right on track by shooting the stars. The key to it was the sextant. When I first started flying with it, there was a little area on top of the aircraft called the astrodome. Judge Roy Hofheinz borrowed the name for his stadium in Houston, I guess. It was a small Plexiglas space on top of the aircraft where you would hang the sextant. The sextant was an instrument probably about twelve inches long and about eight inches wide, with dials and switches on it. If the air became turbulent, I would be standing on a metal table without any sort of flight restraint, trying to shoot the stars with a steady hand while the airplane was pitching and yawing, and the sextant was swinging back and forth. Later, we got into periscopic sextants. With those, I could stand on the deck of the airplane and shoot, because the periscope went all the way up and I could turn it and focus on the stars. The essence of celestial navigation was being able to identify the stars, and at one point I could sit out on a clear night and identify forty celestial varieties of brilliant stars with magnitude enough to easily shoot and rely on. They never failed. The navigator could be wrong, but the stars had been there since the beginning, and in that was the ancient truth of navigation.

The essence of celestial navigation required accurate precomputation. We utilized huge standardized books with table after table of numbers. There were three volumes: two for the northern hemisphere and one for the southern. The navigators would use those to find where they should be. If the wind was performing the way they thought it was going to, and if it was not shifting and everything stayed steady with the air speed and ground speed he figured, the computation should be easy to shoot and rely on. To confirm the computation, though, the navigator would shoot the stars. He would, in effect, go way ahead of the airplane on the charts and estimate the location at a specific time, and then plot what the stars would look like at that time. Then he would start shooting, being careful to check the air speed against what he thought the reading was going to be. That was the trick. That was the mathematical part of the process. If a navigator could do that, once the plane got to that point, he would plot out lines of position for triangulation. Where the lines all came together – that was the position of the plane. It was the gospel truth and there was no reason for it to vary, so we had to accept it. To me, it was so beautiful to do that and to have a complete mission of nothing but celestial reckoning, and then to land and have the instructor say, "That's just terrific. That's wonderful." I was never prouder of my work than at that moment.

Although the pilots and others certainly appreciated the work of the navigator, we could also be considered the butt of some inside-the-service jokes. I remember a conversation years later with R.

Adm. Charles "Chuck" Grojean, who was working with the Museum of the Pacific War in Fredericksburg when I was a commissioner for the Texas Historical Commission. He said to me, "Tom, were you in the navy or the air force?" "I was in the air force, Admiral," I replied. He said, "Well, my pilot friends always said the three most useless things in the world were the runway behind me, the sky below me, and a navigator. What did you do in the air force?" "Well, I was a navigator." "Oh, I'm sorry," he said.[1]

I mentioned the niche of aviation history earlier. Rapid technological advancements in the first decades after World War II meant flight crew members had to constantly deal with change and innovation. When I started, my class designation was BORB (Bomber or Reconnaissance Bomber), so BORB-36 was a B-36. Two months into the training it became BORB-36–47, and about six months later it was BORB-36–47–52, and then they would drop the 36, so that was the progression – from 36 to 47 to 52. Probably within eighteen months it went from the eight-engine pusher, beautiful aircraft, to B-47s and B-52s, with the super jets and all that. The transition to jets really came near the end of my career. I was going to stay in, because I was so fond of it and really liked the discipline. I mean, if I was told to be somewhere at 0800 hours, I was there at 0800 hours. To this day, I get very upset with people who are longtime late, but the world has changed.

I remember that while training at Ellington, for example, most of the flights took off at 0200 or 0300 for some reason. So, I would be driving across Houston, which was a relatively small town in 1953 – bigger than any town I had ever seen, however, and certainly larger than Wellington, Kansas. One of my vivid memories of those days was that while driving out to the base, frequently in the rain, I could pick up American Airlines' "Music till Dawn" show on the radio, and they frequently seemed to be playing Handel. They would most often play the "Water Music" suite or the "Music for the Royal Fireworks" overture, and I never go to Houston or drive through without thinking of that. At the time, every place was dark – no lights on, no streetlights – and mine was the only car on the road. I would get out to the base and have the briefing, go out on a flight for about five hours, come back and debrief, and then go home. That was basically it, but I believe it was that feeling of being able to do something that few other people could do that kept it exciting. I guess there was pride to some extent, but it was not boastful. Rather, it was a pride of personal accomplishment, because I had succeeded against the odds. The training was tough, and at various points I either thought the effort was not worth it or that I might give up, but I never quit. Over time, I got better, and then all the doubts were behind me.

I was not the best navigator, but I survived. There were guys who had been doing it for so long that it was just second nature to them, but I had to study because I did not have a natural proclivity for the process. I have no mechanical ability, either, so I probably had no business being in the training. I really had to fly, though, and I would not give up those memories for the world. It was difficult, because I was not only fighting the system; I was fighting myself. I was resisting, being a lazy guy, and thinking I should have a regular job like other folks. I remember one particular morning when I was coming back from a flight that had not gone well, and I just said to myself, "This is the last time. I'm going to go out there tomorrow and just give it up." When I got home, though, I changed my mind and decided to go back the next day. Like that, I just kept on going and moving forward.

I had help from some of my other trainees, too – some of whom were retreads from World War II. One went by the nickname of "Dad." He was a squadron navigator, a venerable old captain, probably thirty-five years old, and a congenial guy. He would work with me and say, "Tom, you've got to polish up on this stuff. Your dead reckoning is not very good, and that's the key to it all." But he would give me confidence, too. He would say, "You can do this. I know it's hard for you, but you can do this." Dad's flights were just impeccable. His flight logs looked like he had printed them with a typewriter. The logs were all intricate forms. On every flight, the navigator retained the flight plan, where you were at what time, where you thought you were going to be, what your circular error (CE) was, and countless other details. SAC bomber flights were rated on a circular error of target, and a radar bomb site (RBS) would monitor the plane's position. The navigator on a bomber, for example, would talk to personnel on the ground and say, "Bomb release now," and they would check the time and say something like, "OK, you're half a mile off. Circular error one half mile." If the CE was more than two miles, the navigator got in trouble, because they were worried about collateral damage.

Survival school training was an interesting component of SAC. Every combat crew had to go through survival schools, and they included jungle, desert, and mountain environments. I only went through the mountain training for some reason – maybe because I was close to getting out. It was interesting that although we were in the air force, we took the train from Salina, Kansas, to Stead Air Force Base, northwest of Reno, Nevada.[2] We were there, I believe, for a two-week course. The first part of it was just how to survive, and there were demonstrations of interrogation, for example, and how to keep from blabbing everything we knew to enemy interrogators. As the old line goes, we were to tell only our name, rank, and serial number. They had set up a demonstration for about ten of us in a tent. The trainer said, "OK, who wants to volunteer to show you how the interrogation methods might work?" There was this arrogant guy, and he said, "I can do this. Take me." He got up there and sat down, and the interrogator said, "Describe what you see here, Lieutenant." He said, "I see something hooked up to a battery and I see a couple of copper strips. I don't know what you're going to do with those." The trainer said, "Well, I'll show you. Remember, I don't want you to ever say anything more than your name, your rank, and your serial number, so repeat that for me right now, please." The guy did so, and then the trainer continued, "OK, sit down here and put one of these strips in each hand." The interrogator then began cranking the generator. He said, "What's your name?" "So-and-so." "Rank?" "So-and-so." "Outfit?" "So-and-so." "What aircraft are you flying?" "KC-97." "What's your squad?" "407." He told him everything he wanted to know in just a few seconds, while his hair was beginning to stand up. The trainer, a sadistic fellow, kept smiling as he continued to crank. Finally, the guy screamed, "Turn it off! Turn it off! Turn it off!" "My point is made," said the instructor. "If you take this kind of pressure, you're going to crack, and all you can do is hope you don't know anything that's going to aid the enemy." That exercise is one reason I have such respect for the late John McCain, because he endured so much more.

All the men who did this type of training were members of the Aggressor Force, and they all wore green uniforms. They were part of SAC, but I was not sure to whom they reported. They were probably acting to carry out one of LeMay's fixations. They flew their own airplanes. They would come to air bases on alerts, although no one there knew they were coming. We would be in the barracks or wherever, and one plane would come in, usually a C-47, a Goony Bird, and the crew would report to the tower and ask for landing instructions. If the tower operator was not up to it, he would reply, "OK, Air Force 677, take runway 36 and come on in. Headwinds so-and-so, maintain speed such-and-such, taxi," and then he would get a follow jeep out there to bring them in. The pilot would reply and say, "Good deal. Talk to you later, tower." These guys were playing the roles of enemies, of course, so the tower operator unknowingly gave them permission to land. Once they did so, they had a whole plane full of guys in green uniforms who would come pouring out like clowns from a circus car, all carrying weapons, and they threatened to kill anyone who came near them. This was classic LeMay. He had devised this Aggressor Force, and they were deadly. Vicious men. I encountered one of them personally, and several of them in general, and I never saw a single hint of human compassion in any of them. They were these hard-eyed, steel-jawed guys, completely dedicated to what they were doing. They were as dedicated to that as we were to our mission.

When the Aggressor Force took over, they laid down the absolute rules of engagement. One guard in the field with a rifle, for example, was supposed to equal twenty troops, and you had to keep that in mind always. If you encountered him, he was not alone. There were nineteen other mythical aggressors standing there with him, and you could not steal his gun because one of the other nineteen would shoot you, so that was basically it. For the last phase of the exercise, we had nine days in the field, in the Sierra Nevada Mountains during the winter. There was snow on the ground, and we were given snowshoes, which were not much more than tennis rackets in those days. There were silly rules. We got to carry a pound of raw beef and something like ten packs of cigarettes or a pipe, and four packages of pipe tobacco, and all kinds of C-rations and ways to boost the flavor of anything you caught in the field. In theory, we were supposed to be jumping out of an airplane, but they gave that up because it got to be that guys were breaking their legs and otherwise being injured. We jumped out of the back of a truck instead. We were in the field and probably thirty miles from the base itself, way up in the mountains, and our objective was to get back to Stead in a prescribed amount of time. We traveled as a crew and worked our way out of the mountains onto a flat plain that led to Stead, but it was covered with barbed-wire entanglements around everything. They said if we got to that point, though, we were 99 percent free, but they were looking for us, regardless, and planning to capture us. If they had, we would have been treated as prisoners of war and subjected to interrogation. We had partisans to meet and certain rendezvous points to consider, and then we were to build a makeshift runway in a valley in the mountains by using tree boughs as the edge of the runway, and then lighting them when the airplane came over so the crew could see where to land.

We carried a forty-pound pack in addition to everything else, and on occasion we got to carry a radio, which added another ten pounds. In all, we had fifty pounds of supplies, going across snow on snowshoes. We didn't carry any weapons, of course; we were just walking, sometimes with the aid of a makeshift walking stick if there were trees around. We would start off with the snowshoes until they broke through and were worthless under the crust. We had to sit down in the snow and take them off and then put them back on and go as far as we could until they broke through again. We subsisted on the meat we had taken. They gave us a section of parachute nylon, and we would dig a hole and wrap the meat in the silk and put coals on top of it. So, we had to eat cold meat for a while, but over nine days with that kind of exertion, the energy runs out quickly. It helped somewhat that I smoked a pipe, because that tamped down some of the hunger pangs, but I lost forty pounds in nine days regardless. The only wild game we managed to get was a porcupine – a very slow and dumb animal – which was running across the snow, and one of our more agile crew members hit the thing in the nose with a piece of wood. Bump. Instantly dead. He butchered this poor little thing, finally got the quills off, and had a great supply of toothpicks. Once he got him all dressed out, I just looked at it and said, "I can't eat that thing." Egged on by my crew members to eat for survival sake, I finally gave in and ate the liver, which tasted faintly like pine, because that is primarily what the porcupine eats. I have never touched another bite of porcupine liver since that day.

We finally got down to the point where we were to proceed individually once we made it to the last stage. At that point, the land was completely barren. It was a dry lake bed, almost completely devoid of vegetation except for little clumps of brush. It was pitch dark and we could see the air base glowing like a jewel on the horizon. With that, we took off and clambered under the barbed wire while they occasionally fired live machine gun rounds over our heads. We could hear them zinging and could smell them going over. We were going across on our backs, pulling that wire, and then when we got free, there would another barbed-wire entanglement awaiting us. Finally, I got within about a hundred yards of the Promised Land and faced the last wire, and then – *click*! I looked up and there was this guy standing there pointing a rifle at me. He said, "Consider yourself a prisoner of war," and I said, "OK." I was worn out, hungry, and weak, and therefore somewhat relieved. He said, "I'll call and have them come pick you up." It was all deadly serious. This guy, my captor, puts his rifle against the wire and is cranking on his walkie-talkie, and I'm looking at that gun and looking at him, looking at that fence, looking at those lights. He looked at me and said, "Don't even try it," because in theory, there were nineteen other guys there.

The truck eventually came, and fortunately the whole program ended at midnight – it was about 11:45 when I got captured. It had been nine long days. The truck picked me up and got back to base about ten minutes till twelve, and they were shutting it down, so I avoided any interrogation. Instead, they opened the doors, you know, and they had this great big feast going in there – good air force food, big steaks and lots of other things, and man, we just hit that banquet and ate everything to the point we made ourselves sick. Then we got back on the train and headed home.

This training all came back to me years later when I was out driving around in civilian life and ventured down in far West Texas to a historical place called Desert Hot Wells, twenty-four miles or so southeast of Sierra Blanca. It was probably 1971. My car broke down, and I was out in search of civilization. It was a hot day in July – my birthday, in fact. I had not prepared to get lost in such rough country, but I just kept going. I would see a tree and head for that, and then I would sight another tree and just keep pressing forward. I finally got picked up and taken back into town. What I had learned in survival school was a lifesaving lesson, though. I would think, *I cannot go on anymore*, and then immediately I would remind myself, *Well, I just have to make it to that next tree.*

8
The Sheer Moment of Departure

When we were at Brize Norton, we flew demonstration flights over Europe to show off our refueling capabilities and equipment. One of those was to Trondheim, a beautiful town in Norway, which was part of the North Atlantic Treaty Organization (NATO) agreement. There's a huge bay that the Germans had used as a staging area during World War II, and the Royal Air Force (RAF) had raided it quite successfully and destroyed a big piece of the German fleet. Germans had been there a long time, but we could not see much evidence of their presence. One afternoon at the base we were socked in and unable to fly. It was raining and cold, and I headed out by myself for a look around Trondheim. I wanted to see the bay where all this action had taken place, and there was a huge cliff right next to the water. I climbed it and found a cave facing the sea where there had probably been a gun emplacement at one time. There was no entry door, but I could see well enough, so I just walked in, although I had no flashlight. There were shelves of German food that nobody had touched since the war. The Norwegians had so resented the Nazis that they never went in that place. There were canned goods and boxes of supplies, and I was just fascinated. I stayed there for a long time, and I could feel the history just soaking in. What must have happened? Why were these supplies there? Why did the Nazis leave? It was a great experience for someone so interested in history.

Not all our trips were planned so much in advance, nor did they afford us much sightseeing time. I remember one particular New

Year's Eve in Kansas, probably in 1955. We had a briefing in the morning from a Major Munday, who was a retread—a colorful old boy who was bald as a billiard ball and who drove a sports car like LeMay. The major said, "Gentlemen, I have to talk to you about something that I have talked to air force officers about before, and that is the practicing of moderation." He added, "Tonight is New Year's Eve, and I know the proclivity's going to be to celebrate the coming of the new year, and I trust you will take my word for it and practice moderation tonight. We don't want to lose anybody." We all assured him we would, of course. I got to the officers' club, and all the women, including my wife, were done up in their finery—the best they could put on in Kansas. It was about 11:40 that evening when the lights went up and the band stopped playing, and a guy said, "Gentlemen, we've been alerted. We are leaving in twenty minutes. Get to your aircraft as soon as possible. Go to Operations, get your flight gear, get on your aircraft, and get airborne." All the women were put on air force busses and taken home or to our cars. Everybody thought it was an alert, just a joke, and that by the time we got to the end of the runway, we would come back. When we got there, though, we lifted off and kept on going. Our destination was Thule, Greenland, where we stayed for two weeks. Our wives had no idea where their husbands had gone. It was just an alert, but it was also just LeMay at work. He was testing to see if his guys could do it, and the message on moderation had come right from Offutt—right from LeMay's headquarters.

The moderation warning worked well, for the most part, but there was this one aircraft commander—I only remember by his nickname, Spike. He was not commanding my plane, however. He had paid no attention to the moderation advice, and the plane got fired up and everybody was sitting there, and he was at the yoke. As he headed off down the runway for takeoff, he passed out. He just fell forward onto the yoke, but his copilot, a guy out of Texas A&M, was somehow able to push old Spike back in his chair and take that plane off one-handed, narrowly avoiding a disaster.

Secret missions, like that one on New Year's Eve in 1955, were rough on our spouses, mates, and children. Whatever my wife thought the new year would bring in Salina, Kansas, she would never predict me taking off and flying to Greenland. While I was gone, she agonized over what our future might be together. When I returned, she said, "Here's a choice. It's either the air force or me," and I made the wrong choice. I said, "OK, I'll stay with you." I thought we could make it work. Although I had already applied for a regular commission and committed to going on through the college training, and probably would have retired as a lieutenant colonel, I withdrew my application. My last mission was to Nebraska, where we did a refueling demonstration at Offutt Field with Curtis LeMay looking on. It went beautifully.

I was scheduled to depart the service on my birthday in 1956, but shortly before, the 40th Bomb Wing got orders to go to Elmendorf, Alaska, and I obviously could not go because of my exit timing. On the evening of July 10, I sat at the end of the runway in a blue and white Ford coupe and watched them all go. Whew! It was a tough night for me. The departure went off in organized flights. I knew the size of the unit, of course, so I watched and counted as the tankers went first, followed by the B-47s, and I sat there silently as the last one disappeared into the sky. That was the end of SAC for me. I reported the following day, settled my accounts, and turned my back on the experience. I did not sit around and fret about the situation, and I was not remorseful even for a while, but I also never forgot that sheer moment of departure the night before. It symbolized so much for me, personally.

After leaving SAC and having difficulty in landing a job in Denver, we moved to my wife's home state of Illinois, and I worked for the vast Marshall Field operation in Chicago, first as a copywriter and later in marketing. I maintained my military status on inactive reserve, though, flying for the new 108th Refueling Squadron of the Illinois Air National Guard out of O'Hare Airport. I went out there for an interview and met with an officer who had all my records. He said, "Yeah, we can use you. Do you want to sign on?" Without hesitation, I replied, "Yeah, you bet," and I just did it without home approval, shall we say. It was like a second chance—like all of a sudden here was this opportunity to do it again. I dragged out my uniform, which was much too big for me by then, since I had lost a lot of weight. I had to have it altered down, but I had enough stuff to outfit myself as a reasonable-looking air force officer, so I just picked it up and went out there. For my wife, at least, that only exacerbated the problem. We had a daughter, Ann, soon after moving to Chicago, so once again the pressure was on for me to leave the air force. "Can't you just leave those things alone?" she would ask. My response was usually something like, "Well, I've got to do this. It's not technically a long-lasting career in the air force, but I'm going to stay in and do the guard." Truthfully, it was exactly like active duty. There was no line drawn between the guard and active duty, as guard planes refueled SAC planes all over the place. By 1958, the US main military was cutting back. They were beginning to rely on the reserves and the National Guard more and more, and today the reserves and National Guard compose 70 percent of our forces, because they have continued to cut the finances.

With the Illinois Air National Guard, I swore an oath to the governor of the state of Illinois, took all the flight physicals, and began flying as a crew member. I had the credentials, so it was like a leg up. I knew all the equipment and knew how to deal with it, and I had a lot of flying hours. The National Guard, of course, equals the Active Reserve. There was a reserve unit at O'Hare, where they flew the C-119, known as the Flying Coffin. We also flew the brand-new KC-97s that had been built for SAC, but SAC could not take them. LeMay was retired, the military clout in the government was gone, and they were cutting back. The military is, by its nature, extremely competitive. The navy hates the army, the army hates the air force, the navy hates the marines, and so on. President Eisenhower had it in his power, when he created the Defense Department, to do away with the interdepartmental competition and combine it into one service. One of the great moderators that served as an example of how this could work was Texas A&M College (later Texas A&M University). The guys who came out of there went into any branch they wanted, and it worked. Eisenhower chose not to follow that example, though. He was an army man and therefore did not want to see army traditions shot down. He could have consolidated the budgets, and it would have saved the government millions and millions of dollars every hour, but he chose otherwise.

In the Air National Guard (ANG), I reported for duty every other weekend. To take advantage of the pay, we would generally take off at 11:30 on a Friday night and fly all day Saturday, get someplace, stay there on Sunday, and leave early Monday morning and fly back again. That equaled four paid workdays. We were flying KC-97s, ferrying people around early on, and then we went back into straight refueling with SAC, meeting SAC planes anywhere in the world. It was a full-fledged deal. The tails of our aircraft carried the letters ANG, and there are pictures today that document this. There was no animosity between the US Air Force and National Guard whatsoever. There was a seamless transition between the two, and nobody said, "You're National Guard. That doesn't count." We were air force again.

I moved up rather quickly as part of the ANG, and the jump from captain to major was a stupendous step. I got the orders to report to Rantoul, Illinois, headquarters of the Illinois Air National Guard, for the promotion. Moving from captain to major was something like a spot promotion. I was fairly adept at the navigation trade, so I became an instructor, and in that particular unit the instructors were bumped up a grade. I thus went from captain to major in about a year and a half, which is phenomenal.

My new role as instructor came about because I had developed an unusual proficiency for the work. When I started, my mathematics skills were just dreadful, but somehow I was able to create an aptitude where an aptitude did not exist, because I enjoyed it so much. It was the purity of it, because navigators are in concert with the elements. The process is unforgiving, however. It was not like my later profession in retail, where the boss might be impressed with your work or think you might need more training. In navigation, the object is to get the airplane from point A to point B, and that is it. The navigator cannot change that. If he messes up, the consequences might be missing the target, crashing, or getting intercepted by fighter planes, which is embarrassing. That never happened to me, though.

I remember flying a couple of missions with my instructor Dale Olson. One of his reports about my work stands out in my memory. "Captain Alexander," he wrote, "flew an outstanding mission. His ETA was within one second of what he said it was going to be." Circular error was one quarter of a mile off where I said I would take it, but we could see the target, so we were not in trouble. Olson was a squadron navigator and got promoted to lieutenant colonel from major, because it was instructor status. There was only one instructor crew in a unit like that, so when he got promoted and became more of an administrator for the whole outfit, he had to have an instructor. He recommended me for the position, and I interviewed for it with the commanding brigadier general who came out of Rantoul. We interviewed and then scheduled a test flight. The night before that flight I was shaking like a leaf because it had been so long since anybody had looked over my shoulder. This guy was an IBM typewriter salesman trying to sell Marshall Field, and I think that is the reason I got the gig, but I flew a very good mission, so I got the job and became the squadron navigator and the lead navigator.

To me, instructors had the ultimate responsibility. The guys who came in the squadron on the basis that I did were invited by the guard. The air force had published a list of people who had air flight codes (AFC) of 1531 or 1524. The guard then contacted the guys, and they came in. They just kept coming in all the time, and it soon reached full strength shortly after it formed. There were only a few people when I went out there—probably an adjutant, an instructor-navigator, about four pilots, a chief pilot, and a commander—and that was basically it. We probably had about four KC-97s, but they kept coming in. The air force was getting rid of them, as they were going into the jets, like the KC-135, which is a 707 Boeing transformed into a tanker. Big airplane. I only flew in it twice. It was so much different than cranking those engines. As the unit continued to grow and more and more personnel came in, those with the best ratings stood out for recognition. At first, I was one of maybe four navigators in Major Olson's training class, but I was on test flights all over the United States and getting rated in the process. Pretty soon I was better than the other guys, so when Olson moved up, I also moved up and took his place. Being an instructor gave me a feeling of being useful, because I was imparting information I had learned primarily through experience. It was one of the greatest rewards ever.

Navigation training took on new dimensions in the decade after World War II, particularly with the increased reliability of radar. Still, as instructors, we also needed to teach the basics of celestial navigation while keeping the plane on track. As we would often say of the aircraft commanders behind their backs, they were simply truck drivers. We had to tell them where to go, though. We had to get them to the mission point and then back. "Fat, dumb, and happy" was the expression. Anybody could land an airplane, we thought, but only special people could shoot a star and get you from point A to point B.

Instructing had its downfalls, though. I have flown with trainees who would just panic under the pressure, but I had to work them through those situations. I could not let it get to the point where I had to take over. While the trainee worked it out, though, the plane might be meandering through the sky, seemingly lost. At that point, the aircraft commander might look back at me, seeking direction, but I would just point to the trainee. I had to leave him alone and see if he could make the necessary corrections. On occasion, that misdirection could put us in danger. All over the country they had closely-patrolled Aircraft Identification Zones (ADIZ), and fighters were ready to scramble anytime something penetrated those areas. Once we were flying with a trainee who headed us straight to an ADIZ. I said, "Bill, do you think you're doing OK here?" He said, "Leave me alone." When we got to the point where we actually penetrated the zone, I had no recourse but to take over. I said, "We're out of here," and called for a ninety-degree turn. It was too late, though, as the ground crew had been notified and responded with a fighter for a visual identification. They would not accept a radio identification at that point, of course. On this occasion we got intercepted, and all hell broke loose when we got back. It was absolutely a cardinal sin.

The aircraft commander was furious. I think he was angry with me too, because I had failed to stop the guy. I just thought that surely he would realize his mistake, because radar was painting this picture and we could see incredible detail. For example, San Francisco is probably the perfect radar return, because radar does not pick up water. You thus get this vast black space, and here is this city just spread out, where you can clearly see the bridges. Denver, Colorado, was also that way—the whole black western part of the state had nothing. Mountains would kind of show up, and here would be this big bright blob on the radar. It was just inviolate. ADIZs probably still exist around test grounds, firing ranges, and sites like that, but tensions were particularly high with the Cold War in the 1950s. There was the pervasive fear that "the Russians are coming." It was the era of mutual destruction—in effect, if you are going to blow us up, we are going to blow you up first.

All of that—the weekend missions, the secrecy, the uncertainties, and the Cold War dangers—did not sit well back home. My wife and I were living on a farm outside St. Charles, Illinois, west of Chicago, that is now a large residential subdivision. We only had one car, which was the norm in those days, and my wife would take me to the Northwestern rail line so I could commute downtown, do my work, and commute back. It ended up I was making more money with the guard part-time on those long weekends. I would volunteer for the weekend jaunts to pick people up. It was mainly ferrying—taking an old plane out to Boeing in Seattle and getting a new one and flying it back.

I enjoyed my time at Marshall Field, but I enjoyed my time with the guard even more. I was the only Marshall Field employee in the guard at that time, but there was never a discussion at work about my weekend service and I never talked to my boss about it. There was a time during the Cuban missile crisis where someone asked where I had been, but I just replied, "I can't tell you." Eventually, I got the "bug" again and applied to go back into the service. I had not alerted my wife about my decision, but then I received the acceptance letter ordering me to report to Lowry Air Force Base near Denver and I had to let her know. She said, "You simply cannot do it, for the sake of Ann. For the sake of our daughter, you can't go risking your life." Our personalities and ambitions were totally different. I really wanted to be this career officer, and she did not want to be a career officer's wife. Following a subsequent move to Houston, our marriage finally ended in divorce in 1963.

9
Cuba

While I was with the National Guard, I remember the night President Kennedy made his speech about the Soviet Union moving missiles into Cuba. I was watching television with my daughter, who was about six at the time. We were sitting there on the sofa together, and I said, "Well, there goes your daddy." She looked up and said, "What do you mean?" I said, "Just wait a couple of days and then you'll find out." The next day or two, sure enough, I got my orders. The squadron commander was a regular air force lieutenant colonel who, like many in the service, did not necessarily love war but seemed to have a need for it. Some airmen knew they were not going to be promoted without being able to prove their ability seriously, and of course SAC tested people all the time, but this guy wanted those federal hours—those activated hours—and he got his wish when we got the gig to fly to Wake Island. He called me and said, "Alex, we've got to go. I've volunteered." We were to be the lead crew on the mission." I said, "OK," and then he added, "Don't tell anybody, but we've got to leave." With that, I just got up and walked out of my office. I shared the space with another guy, and I said, "I've got to go, Bob." When he asked what was up, I simply said, "It's air force stuff that I can't tell you about, but I'm going." My boss was out of town at the time, so I couldn't tell him. The communications were not like they are today—no email and no cell phones. I went home and went out to the base from there. My wife took me out there, because we still only had one car. I did not get much additional information when I checked in, except that we might be gone two to three weeks. With that, we took off.

I was an instructor on this lead crew, and I had a student navigator on board named Bill Cleveland. Bill was a big, affable Idahoan, I think—just a great big, bucolic farm kid who I thought was going to be a pretty good navigator. I was getting in hours watching him work. I did not have to do anything at all except watch him and make sure he did not get too far off course. So, we took off and headed to Travis Air Force Base in California, just outside of San Francisco. We sat out there waiting to be alerted, to go get this mission, and it was to fly to Wake Island, pick up a detachment of marines, and ferry them back to the states and then to Homestead Air Force Base in Florida. Located near Miami, the base is inactive now, but it was the staging area for the possible invasion of Cuba. All available military personnel were scrambling to get to Homestead. As we waited for our alert at Travis, the skies were just buzzing with activity, and there was an unmistakable electricity in the air that I never felt any other time, because I never was that close to combat. Although we had no specific details at the time, we knew we were going to do something that was directly related to the Cuban crisis.

We sat around Travis for about two days, I guess. It was a fascinating experience. Instructors like us all wore orange flight suits, which were pretty colorful, and we were mixed in with first lieutenant marine fighter pilots in the officers' club. We guardsmen were primarily old guys in our thirties, and there was a whole bunch of air force guys called back up, all waiting for something to happen. In our minds we saw the Russians coming with their weapons, and we were getting armed, ready to go. The tension in that club was interesting, because everybody wanted to go—particularly the marines. I have said this before, and I always get in trouble for it, but marines are a little bit nuts and fighter pilots are nuts, so a marine fighter pilot is a very unusual character. They can be arrogant and cocky, but they are good at what they do. While we waited, we all drank to ease the tension. One day we got a notice to prepare for takeoff, but we taxied out to the runway and just held in place. The next morning, to clear our heads, we used oxygen masks out at the end of the runway, just to get over the hangover, and soon we would get to the point where we felt much better. While prudent minds might have argued for complete sobriety, the tension was just immense. To be fair, no one was drinking to the point that they were out of control. Instead, they were testing themselves to see if they were able to function. We would just go out there and wait, engines running full speed, until we heard "It's a no go" from the tower, and we would go back around and head to the officers' club, starting our routine all over again.

The reasons for an aborted flight could vary—perhaps the marines were not ready or another plane was picking up a different function. It was a scramble to get everything organized, because it was the first crisis since the advent of the Vietnam War and it seemed imminent. Eventually, though, we got the green light, and off we went. Well into the first leg of the flight to Hickam Field in Honolulu, I remember we were the only plane in sight. We were droning along on a beautiful day in a clear sky, and we could look down to the Pacific Ocean and see ships moving along. I was looking out the window and watching this magnificent scene, and suddenly Cleveland said, "Tom, I can't do this." I asked, "What do you mean you can't do this?" We are hundreds of miles off the California coast and he is unable to continue? He said, "I just can't take the responsibility for this." He panicked a bit. "Well, I tell you what," I said, "Go back and sit down, just take it easy, and I'll take it over." I told the captain, and he said, "Do whatever you have to do."

Without GPS and not yet in range of radar, we were sort of on our own. It was just us, the sky, God, Boeing, and the Pratt and Whitney engines. "Go back and sit down, and I'll figure it out," I told Cleveland. Unfortunately, his map, his chart, and his log were just terribly confused. Somehow, I was able to rectify the situation and figure out where we should have been, and I was shooting stars because night had come. Finally, I came up with an ETA into the Hawaiian Islands, Oahu, and then Hickam Field. Soon, we picked up the radar blip way off in the left-hand corner of the screen. I knew it was not a wooden ship and realized it had to be something big, like a land mass. We were flying along and getting closer and closer to it; then suddenly the IFF blip noted it was Hickam Field, and we were two hundred and some miles out. I just maintained that course—I had gotten us back on track and back on time, and I will never forget we flew over what I assumed to be the coastline of Hawaii and there were bonfires all along on the ground. We were coming in on final approach into

Hickam, so they were on Oahu, I guess. I thought, what in the world? I always wondered why they were there, but regardless, it was one of the most wonderful sights I had ever seen. I could not see any people, but I could see these flickering flames, and pretty soon Honolulu came into sight, and then Pearl Harbor and Hickam Field.

At the end of the flight, Lieutenant Cleveland came up to me and said, "I'm so sorry. I don't know what happened to me." I said, "OK, Bill, we'll take care of it." And the aircraft commander came back, and asked, "What's with him?" I said, "I don't know. I can't answer that, but I'll take care of it." He replied, "You're going to fly back. I'm not going to trust him going back the other way." I said OK. We all went out on the town and milled around for about a day, and then found out we were getting ready to go. I was staying at the BOQ, our Bachelor Officers' Quarters. On the morning of our departure for Wake Island there was a knock on the door. I opened it and there was Bill Cleveland, and he looked like a pumpkin. He had eaten a papaya, and the papaya had somehow affected him, giving him this great big orange face. He looked like a lantern. "What's happened to you?" I asked. "I don't know. I ate some fruit and I'm just sick." We got him to Tripler Medical Hospital right on Oahu and sat in the waiting room with him. Meanwhile, the plane was getting about five hours from takeoff and I was the only navigator, so I had to get there and do the preflight. I am sitting there with my student, the only national guardsman there from Illinois, in the waiting room with all these other local military guys waiting to get into the military hospital—a sometimes daunting task. Finally, Cleveland got called, and I said to the intern, "I've got to go. I can't stay here." "We'll take care of him," he assured me. "Don't worry about it." I never heard from the guy again. He just seems to have dropped out of sight, but he was a great point of discussion for many, many months.

Regardless, we proceeded with our mission. I was the instructor-navigator on the log, but I was doing the work, and we started flying toward Wake Island, which is about the size of an ant's ear. It's the tiniest little thing, and it required skilled navigation to get to it, because nobody was going to help me. It was just me and my capability to shoot stars and to shoot the sun and compute dead reckoning across this vast body of water. Finally, I picked up Wake, exactly where I had hoped it would be. It was a little tiny blip and a coral atoll of less than three square miles—essentially just a landing strip. When I saw the blip, I called ahead and said something like, "Wake Island, this is Air Force 2730 inbound." They, of course, knew who we were because we had passed all the ADIZs getting in. We landed and were on the ground in only about eight hours. I was just worn out, so I went to the BOQ and slept until the briefing for the return. We picked up the marines, who were always the most disciplined guys. They walked with purpose, chins tucked in, as if they were marching to the plane. They sat in the back, and there were very few provisions back there for passengers. Additionally, the seats were just hard metal with straps over the top, and we could accommodate only around twenty. Other planes were coming in to pick up the rest of them.

On our first leg back from Wake, we flew into Hickam Field in Hawaii, because that plane lacked the range to go all the way to California. As we were landing, the number-three engine went out and just flat flamed. It seemed like it was always the number-three engine on the KC-97 that caused trouble for some reason. The plane will not perform properly with three engines, so we offloaded the marines to a C-124 Air Transport Command plane heading to the states. With them off our hands, we were stuck in Waikiki Beach for about three days while they shipped a part to us out of Kelly Field in Texas.

With the repairs done, we started our second leg to the California coast, but this time without any marines. We were flying an empty plane. As we made our approach to Travis, something happened that had never happened to me before or since. There are a series of islands called the Farallon Islands, far off the West Coast. The approach made a perfect radar picture with the islands, the bay, and the mountains beyond. I gave an ETA to penetrate the ADIZ going into the continental United States, and suddenly the plane stopped. Its progress over the ground stopped. Usually, the wind blew in toward the shore, but on this occasion, it was blowing back out at a tremendous clip. As a result, the plane literally stopped. We were not going very fast, about 280 knots or something, as fast as a tanker would go, and the wind had to be some immense reverse jet stream to have paralyzed that airplane. I was looking at the radar and noticed nothing was moving. We were just churning in the sky. I called the aircraft commander and said, "Colonel, we've got a problem. This thing isn't going anywhere." "What do you mean?" I said, "Look at your radar scope." He had a little tiny one up front, and when he looked at it, he replied, "What in the hell is this?" "I don't know," I admitted. He called the ADIZ, and I heard him say, "You're not going to believe this, but we're marooned. We're stuck; we cannot come in. We're hanging out here just like we're hanging out laundry." The ADIZ radio operator replied, "We've had a report of that before, earlier this afternoon." We had no choice but to keep going. Our over-the-ground speed was probably fifty miles an hour in a two-hundred-knot aircraft. Eventually, it made enough progress despite our limited fuel to get to Travis, and we landed safely, although the engine was faltering again. It was an air force base, though, so they had the supplies to repair it in a few days.

Once we were cleared for flight, we headed off to O'Hare in Chicago. About two hundred miles from O'Hare, though, the number-three engine conked out again, and the prop was just windmilling. The pilot feathered the prop, and we went along fairly well before the number-one engine started acting up. We had put a lot of strain on that plane, because our course was a long way for a plane like that to fly. It stressed everything. The aircraft commander called the base and said, "We have a slight emergency here." We were coming into the busiest commercial airport in the world, O'Hare, and we were landing this giant military plane right in the middle of it. With emergency conditions, the idea was to warn the commercial flights, because the wounded plane had priority. Somehow, while this was going on, a Chicago radio station picked up the news of the plane in distress headed for O'Hare and alerted people to avoid the area and to expect flight delays. My wife was in our car coming out to pick me up—the base had notified families that the guys were coming back—and she heard the broadcast. Despite that, she made it on out to the field to pick me up. Upon landing, we were surrounded by air force personnel and by bystanders who fired questions at us. "Just what in the world went on? Where have you been?" Of course, we were not allowed to say. When I got back home, I rested up for a couple of days. I had cut my foot while surfing in Hawaii, so when I returned to work I was limping and had a suntan, even though it was December. My boss asked, "Tom, where in the hell have you been? We were so worried about you." I said, "Well, sir, I can't tell you." He said OK and took no further action about it.

Despite the intrigue, by the time I got back to Chicago, the Cuban missile crisis was over and the military was standing down. The marines we picked up at Wake Island finally got to Homestead, I assume, but of course there was no invasion. They just dispersed them all back to where they should be. When I think of all the SAC tensions, here was the moment of truth. While all interest was on Cuba, though, the air force kept thinking it might just be the time the Soviets were going to come over the top and get us, because we were looking the other way. There was this pervasive feeling they were going to sneak up on us. The surveillance carried on over to the north, and I do not know if the Soviets ever tried to penetrate there or not, but the tension had reached a point where we assumed the time of mutual destruction might be at hand.

10
Flyover

Sometime after our activation for the Cuban missile crisis, John F. Kennedy came to Chicago to shore up Mayor Dick Daley's support. The president was flying in and out of O'Hare, specifically our military space of the airport for security purposes. We knew he was coming, and word went out. It happened to be over lunch-break time, and we all went to see him and were standing around. Air Force One—a beautiful plane and a great symbol—was sitting out there. As the motorcade approached, it came up right beside us, and we formed a circle around the president. Many pilots within the guard unit were unhappy with their commander in chief because he had activated them in 1961 in response to the crisis in Berlin. I will never forget that circle of stone-faced officers surrounding the president of the United States, who carried a fedora in his hand. One of his crew members in the navy was president of the Hat Corporation of America, and he convinced his buddy Jack Kennedy to at least carry one of his products to help promote sales. Fedora in hand, he just looked around at everybody's faces slowly and carefully. He went all the way around, and there was not a sign of emotion, nor a cheer, nor a sound of unhappiness—as if the whole thing was frozen in time. He just walked around with a Secret Service agent, and I looked up on top of the hangars and could see more agents standing up there with their weapons. The pilots fired up the engines on Air Force One, and out came the ramp going up to it. The president walked out to the end of the ramp, hat in hand, and looked around and kind of shrugged, like "What have I gotten into here?" He got in the plane and we watched it take off, and that was it. I was probably within six feet of him. I had no quarrel with him myself, although I had not voted for him, but it was an interesting episode.

While I was still in the guard, I once again considered making application for regular air force duty. My rank would not have carried over, but I was given enough time and hours that I probably could have gone in as a major. Based on my job experience at Marshall Field, however, I got a job offer in Houston. It was to be a sales promotion manager of Joske's, part of Allied Stores, an offshoot of the world-famous store operation in San Antonio. It was then a tire and battery store, primarily, with some apparel, and they wanted to upgrade it, so my job was to transform it from an automotive supply store into a fashion store, which was rather challenging. Consumers had strong opinions about this lowball store, where everything was off-price all the time. It was a big job offer that about tripled my salary, but by accepting the position I had to give up the guard. I decided to resign my active duty commission. I stayed on inactive reserve, however, until 1972—a total of nineteen years. Adding the four years of ROTC, that made twenty-three years of military service.

The air force retired me as a captain, which is how my discharge papers read. I had enjoyed a temporary promotion to major, and in fact, the guy whose place I took gave me his gold leaves. When I left the air force, I had no more relations with the service until a few years later. I went from Houston to Seattle with another Allied Stores unit, and while in Seattle I received an offer from Stanley Marcus to go with Neiman Marcus, which is the top of the barrel. I had to accept; even though Seattle is a beautiful place, I really wanted to get back to Texas. In my first year with Neiman Marcus, I received a letter from the air force stating, "We're bringing a squadron of KC-97s into Hensley Field Naval Air Station," which was between Fort Worth and Dallas near Grand Prairie. "We are looking for qualified navigators to come out and man these aircraft," the letter went on, inquiring about my interest in the assignment. I was simply dying to do it, of course, but I was unable to take the assignment because I was traveling so much for Neiman's, and I feared Stanley Marcus would fire me if I broached the subject with him. I started off as sales promotion director for Neiman Marcus and eventually ended up as executive vice president of marketing for the whole corporation. Needless to say, I wisely chose to stay with my business career, but my decision to turn down the Hensley assignment sadly marked the end of my air force career.

During my seventeen-year stint with Neiman Marcus, I bought a ranch along the Erath-Comanche county line near the town of Alexander. Being a rancher fulfilled my childhood dreams and my passion for John Wayne movies, I guess. I had always wanted to have a ranch and deal with cows. It was truly a great experience. While at Neiman's I also met Capy Kromer, who was from the Panhandle and shared my keen interest in the Palo Duro Canyon area. Long after I left Dallas for full-time work at the ranch, and after the death of my second wife, Capy and I met up again. We had a date in Fort Worth. I came up from the ranch and she came over from Dallas. The moment I saw her, I thought, man, this is it. She felt the same way. There was no question about it. That was twenty-six years ago, so it worked out well. I eventually gave up the ranching business, on which I was spending a fortune. The old saying is that the way to make a small fortune in a ranch is to start with a large fortune. It was, indeed, a costly venture. I had almost five hundred acres and was running seventy-five cattle. I was all by myself on the place for about eight years—just a hermit. I would go into town and get supplies and then come back out. Finally, I had a golden retriever and a black cat, and they were my comrades, and all three of us would sleep in the bed, with the cat on one side and the dog on the other. I experienced what may have been one of the coldest winters in that area when it got down to nine below zero. I was out there in the morning in all of the snow, ice, and sleet, dealing with a huge bunch of hungry animals. I had to get the hay out to them on a tractor, and I used a nine-pound maul to break the ice on the frozen ponds. As soon as I did, some stupid cow would walk out into the pond and stand there until the ice reformed around her legs, so I would have to break the ice again to rescue her. Life was tough out there. Someone had to really know something about what they were doing to single-handedly run an operation like that. I put the ranch on the market, thinking it would never sell, but it went quickly and I moved away. Capy and I married soon after and moved to Fredericksburg.

When we were living in Gillespie County, I got the idea from a magazine advertisement to work on a graduate degree from American Military University in Virginia. The list of courses was like a feast to my eyes: Indian Wars, the Mexican War, the Civil War, and right down the line. Capy agreed with me that I just had to do it, so I started and took a double load. I got out of there in eighteen months with a master's degree and honors in Civil War Studies. A little while later I applied for a political appointment to the Texas Historical Commission. By then, I had written a couple of books about airfields in Texas during World War II: *The Stars Were Big and Bright*, volumes one and two. In these volumes I identified the airbases and told the stories of how they came to be, the impact they had on their communities, and how they closed. I got to the point where I was fascinated with the stories. I would go out to West Texas and find an American Legion or a VFW post, and go in and sit at the bar. I had a membership in each, so I could get away with it. Most of the men initially ignored me, but after a day or two someone might ask, "What are you doing here?" "Well, I'm writing a book about the old airbase out here. You know anybody who knows anything about that?" The old-timer would reply, "Yeah, there are a bunch of guys that married local girls when they were stationed here, and they came back and are here all the time. How long are you going to be around?" I would generally reply, "Oh, a couple of days." I would return the next day and there would be four or five guys waiting for me. As long as I bought them a beer, they would share their stories. I have long felt that if a veteran tells you a story, you can assume it happened to him, or maybe it happened to somebody he knew, because the stories are too imaginative to be false. As a result, I used a lot of their anecdotes and perspectives in the books. That became my next career, and it was all-consuming. There is nothing I would rather do than research and write a book.

While I was working on my books, Capy became active in the local Republican Party and attended the state conventions as well. In a receiving line she had the opportunity to speak with Gov. Rick Perry. Being my wife and trained in public relations, she said, "Governor, I have a book you ought to read." Perry said, "What is it?" She replied, "My husband writes these books about abandoned airfields in Texas." Perry is an air force guy, and so he said, "I've flown into a lot of those." She promised to send him a copy of my first book, and she did. About a week later I got a phone call from the governor of the state of Texas, and he said, "Tom, I got your book and I'm really enjoying it. I can't put it down. I want you to send me an invoice and I'll pay you for it." I declined, he thanked me, and that was it. I had already applied for an appointment to the Texas Historical Commission and been passed over, so I called the governor's appointment secretary and asked about reapplying. She said, "Wait a year and resubmit, and if anything has changed along the way, we'll reconsider it." In the meantime, the appointment person changed, and I sent in basically the same application as before, but in the meantime, I had written two more books and been honored by the San Antonio Conservation Society with a publication award. This time around, the interview was totally different. The appointment secretary asked, "How in the world did you make that transition from air force to Neiman Marcus to ranching to writing books? I have to find out how you did that." I said, "Well, I don't know. I just wanted to do it all, and it just came along." She replied, "You've had more careers than most people have coats." At that point I figured I had it, and then she called me about a month later and said, "I was talking to Governor Perry today, and he said, 'I know Tom; put him on the commission.'" I had not had that access the first time.

When I was appointed a THC commissioner, I began to follow up on my concern that the economic, social, and political aspects of World War II had not been recognized fully by Texas. It is likely kind of an unwritten rule that fledgling commissioners, like freshman senators, are not supposed to say anything their first year. I violated that code, though, and made a presentation at a commission meeting in Fort Worth, proposing that we launch a major World War II commemoration. I made the pitch in a committee meeting, and commissioner Shirley Caldwell of Albany was a champion of the idea and really picked up on it. I will never forget when we were later at one of those wonderful dinners at the governor's mansion and she said, "Governor, have you met Tom? He hit the ground running." I thought that was a great introduction. With Shirley's enthusiasm, the support of chairman John Nau, the good work of Cynthia Beeman, and particularly the work of Dan Utley of the agency staff, we started on the initiative immediately. I take great pride in what we accomplished in a short amount of time. There was a lot of fundraising and planning, but it all came together with a memorable event at the Capitol in Austin in 2005. Central to that idea was an image I had of a B-17 leading a flight of various smaller aircraft. The big event was to occur on September 2, the sixtieth anniversary of the signing of the instrument of surrender in Tokyo Bay. I had a vision of the B-17 flying up Congress and over the Texas Capitol. For some reason, though, it came from the other direction. It was dramatic nonetheless. The governor and I were on the platform outside the main entrance, and I was nervously searching the skies for the planes that I thought would be approaching from the south. Suddenly, though, there was a tremendous roar as the planes flew overhead from the north. I received word that for an additional two hundred dollars they would turn around and fly back over from the south, and I said, "I'll pay the two hundred." That was my contribution to the World War II initiative kickoff. It was worth every penny—and more. There was a lot of proud symbolism in that flyover for the war veterans and their families, for historians and history enthusiasts, and for all Texans, including a particularly appreciative onetime stargazing navigator of the Strategic Air Command.

Afterword

Around the Campfire

Dan K. Utley

Back when Tom Alexander was a commissioner of the Texas Historical Commission and I was the staff historian, he sent me a quote that meant a great deal to me, both as a chronicler of the past and as someone who enjoyed his personal reminiscences of the history he has lived. I have collected meaningful or inspirational quotes for decades, so the gift from friend to friend was appropriate, but this particular one was so special that I put it on my office wall, where I could recall it from time to time. Fourteen years and four offices later, it is still by my desk, offering me encouragement and perspective. Attributed to Spenser Abbott, it reads: "We are in a sense still gathered around the campfires, telling each other stories, wondering what's out there in the dark. And we still do not know. We still cannot see beyond the pale cast of the flickering light." Each time I paused to reflect on those lines, I made a mental note to track down Abbott someday to learn more about the context of his words. In preparing this afterword to Major Alexander's adventures, I felt the time had come, but the quest proved somewhat daunting—for, you see, the words represent a quote from the future. In effect, they have not yet been read or written. Let me explain. Science-fiction writer Jack McDevitt used the words as an epigraph in his 2002 novel *Chindi* and sourced them as the work of Abbott from a 2201 publication entitled *Bending the Symmetries*. I will leave the literary analysis of all that for someone else, but the fact remains that I still like the words and find comfort in their personal meaning. They represent just one more debt I owe my friend, Tom Alexander.

The major's military memories appropriately and poignantly ended with the final words of chapter 10, as we planned in our collaboration. Press editors and peer reviewers suggested we move beyond that final scene to a point where Tom could look back and reflect on what the stories in this book now mean to him. Our first effort in that regard was an additional oral history recording, but, while genuine and heartfelt, once translated to the flat plane of paper, it lacked the personality of the previous chapters. Thus, instead, we close with excerpts of that additional text to offer the reader the sense of perspective others recommended.

Having known Tom Alexander for more than a decade, I understand his reticence to place himself in a historical context. Still, there is no denying that he lived through an interesting part of our collective history and that his vivid memories speak strongly to a sense of time and place that still needs elaboration. When we started on this book endeavor together, with the full blessing and support of his beloved wife, Capy, Tom was living on a Kerrville hilltop with a commanding view of the Texas Hill Country. As we worked on the last interview, though, the landscape had changed dramatically. Capy was no longer there, and the commanding view was from a Boulder, Colorado, condominium overlooking the Flatirons. As Tom described, "I now live only a short distance from Folsom Field at the University of Colorado, where my story formally began with the presentation of my military commission sixty-six years ago. I have been many places around the world in the interim," he added, "but I am now back at the beginning, which I suppose is a good way to end a book."

Asked to reflect on his memories of that early air force career, Alexander spoke of both pride and discipline. "I don't remember the shock of that moment when the bars went on the uniform . . . but as time went on, I would wake up in the mornings on a base and put on the uniform or flight suit, and I knew exactly what I was going to do that day. . . . There was something symbolic in that, something that meant I was part of the best." Later, in his post–air force lives of retail and ranching, he experienced similar pride in his work with Neiman Marcus and on his own land, where, he recalled, "It was essentially me against nature."

On his West Texas ranch in Erath and Comanche counties, Alexander recalled that his uniform consisted of neither khaki uniforms nor Brioni suits, but of faded blue jeans, boots, a cowboy hat, and leather gloves. "To some extent," he reflected, "I always felt like I was playing a movie role. I was so inspired by Westerns as a young kid, as far back as Ken Maynard, Tom Mix, Buck Jones, and, of course, John Wayne. When I put on the rancher outfit, I convinced my inner self that I looked a lot like him." The reality failed to meet the perception, though. "I would swagger out and some bull would come up behind and nudge me from the back, and I would think, *Hell, I'm not John Wayne at all*."

Whatever task came his way in his various careers, Alexander utilized the skill sets and character determinants he first honed during his SAC experience, although he often made no direct connections at the time. Some were more evident than others, though—like teamwork and mission focus. "I learned in SAC that the survival of the mission relied heavily on that shared delivery of the team. The pilots had to fly the plane, the navigator had to get the plane to where it was supposed to be, and the navigator-bombardier had to drop a payload." In the era of conventional aircraft, he added, there were also the engineers, radio operators, and others, including ground teams. "All had a role to play, and the role was to complete the mission." Over it all was the "specter of the entire SAC structure," Curtis LeMay. "If you failed the mission, you failed SAC and you failed LeMay, and your future was pretty dim."

In that regard, the transition from aircraft to retail stores seemed minimal at times. "I could take Curtis LeMay's face off his body and slap Stanley Marcus's face back on, and it was about the same. Stanley, like the general, was a perfectionist. I worked at his pleasure. If he wanted to get rid of me, he could do so. He was a one-man personnel office. He could hire you and he could fire you without a moment's notice, and LeMay was very much the same way." Working for himself as a rancher, Alexander found less obvious correlation with his SAC training. "It was not like I thought, 'Gee, Tom, you're really using those good habits you picked up in SAC.'" Regardless, it was all part of a continuum of growth and development that had its foundation firmly established in the air force. "They are characteristics that are part of your actual coloration. I was never consciously emulating LeMay or Marcus." John Wayne, maybe, but not LeMay or Marcus.

As a commissioner of the Texas Historical Commission, Alexander again partnered with powerful colleagues, like chairman John L. Nau III, of Houston, and Shirley Caldwell, of Albany. "I could easily add Nau to that list of LeMay and Marcus," Alexander confided. "He was a guy you did not want to fail. I guess he castigated some people, but a word of praise from John Nau was like the French Croix de Guerre. You really felt like you had accomplished something. He was not an easy man to please. He had very high standards, and in my case at least, I just wanted to live up to his expectations. Working for that guy was a great pleasure." Commissioner Caldwell set high standards as well and was not afraid to speak her mind. "She was a firebrand, and I have seen her go after people like state senators and famous authors. I remember one time she got onto some guy who was an author and who was full of himself, presenting his books as something every schoolchild in Texas should read." She shot back, "'Now, why would you want to do that?' With that, she effectively tied him up, and he was basically mute the rest of the evening."

Despite his various successes, Alexander always carries with him a sense of regret about his truncated time with SAC. He knows he made his decision to leave the service on his best analysis of the situation at the time, but still, he added, "I would not have minded ending my career with those eagles on my shoulder, or maybe even a star. Back in my day, unless you were a pilot, you rarely ever got to be a general. That changed with time, though, and the air force eventually realized being a pilot was not a requisite for being a commanding officer."

Asked to reflect on what his SAC time story might mean for others, particularly young people interested in military service, the major noted, "This may sound like a Horatio Alger part of the book, but part of my SAC takeaway is that as soon as it is possible, I think every young person should get an idea of what it is he or she wants to do. With that in mind, I think they should then hone the skills they are going to need to accomplish that goal." Acknowledging he lived in something of a Norman Rockwell world, albeit one shaken up by World War II and the ensuing Cold War, he greatly values the role of his family in his personal journey. "Somehow out of that, with my parents' support and that of a grandmother, who kept saying, 'You can do better than this,' I persevered." Short of that, he observed, an individual may have to do that on their own. "There are times when you have to push yourself until you feel content, or at least partially content, that you have gone as far as you can go. Then, take the next step and keep moving forward as you are mentally and physically able to do so."

Speaking as a historian capable of some objective self-analysis, historically speaking, and calling for a broader spectrum of resources, Alexander reemphasized the value of the common man as one viable means of understanding greater themes of history. "It is important to state again that if my story has a measure of historical importance, it is not because it is unique in and of itself but rather because it is normal. While it is normal," he was careful to note, "the fact that it has been recorded and preserved through the methodology of oral history gives it a unique value as a document that can be studied, interpreted, and compared with others over time. Through oral history transcripts and other primary sources like photographs and diaries, the normal becomes extraordinary with well-planned preservation and accessibility."

Continuing on about the theme of the historical value of remembered history, Alexander reflected on "what might have happened" under different circumstances. "I served with honor and received an honorable discharge. I did not ever have a bad officer efficiency report. I think I performed what I was supposed to. My only lament is that I wish I could have done more. If there had been an opportunity to prove my mettle in the sense of a trying condition to see if I could measure up to it, I would have, but looking back I regret that I was not tested more, because I would have liked to have seen if I could have met that challenge." The distance of time, he was quick to add, causes one to make such observations. It is part of the process of fitting one small piece of tile into a grand mosaic along with other pieces of the past. "What I did, I did honestly in the context of the time, and I would not change much in that regard. I have thought about this a lot lately and searched my soul, and I think I served with merit. For nobody else's purpose at all, though, I wish I could look at a Distinguished Service Cross or an Air Medal and say, 'Man, did I distinguish myself among my fellow officers?' I never did something that warranted such an award, though, and I reflect on that to this very day."

You, the reader, having followed the personal navigations of a Cold Warrior, can now reflect on that with him. Is a medal the test, or is it the service in a time of national need? Or, is it simply the mission? Other stories of SAC time combined with this one will answer those questions and many others. For those in the games of preservation or the pursuit of history from the bottom up or the inside out, perhaps the time is right. After all, we're not too far removed from the campfire.

Notes

Chapter 3

1. For more information on the Maceo brothers and crime in Galveston, see "Two Brothers and Gaming over Gulf Waters," in Baker, T. Lindsay, *Gangster Tour of Texas* (College Station: Texas A&M University Press, 2011), 309–19.

Chapter 4

1. Thomas E. Alexander, *The Stars Were Big and Bright: The United States Army Air Forces and Texas during World War II*, vol. 1 (Austin: Eakin Press, 2000), 51.

Chapter 5

1. The 1955 movie *Strategic Air Command*, directed by Anthony Mann and based on a screenplay by Beirne Lay Jr. and Valentine Davies, starred James Stewart as Lt. Col. Robert "Dutch" Holland and June Allyson as his wife, Sally. Notable character actors included Frank Lovejoy, Barry Sullivan, Rosemary DeCamp, and Harry Morgan.

2. Falun, Kansas, is a dispersed agricultural community located southwest of Salina and southeast of the Smoky Hill Weapons Range in Saline County. The 2018 population was calculated as 285. See "KS Hometown Locator," http://kansas.hometownlocator.com, accessed February 23, 2019.

Chapter 6

1. The Strategic Air Command utilized Sidi Slimane Air Base, located in the northern part of Morocco, for the forward deployment of bombers during the Cold War.

Chapter 7

1. Charles "Chuck" D. Grojean (1923–2008) graduated from the US Naval Academy in 1945 and enjoyed a distinguishing career in naval operations, serving from 1969 to 1971 as the Commander of NATO Submarine Forces. He later served with the Department of Defense and the Joint Chiefs of Staff, and the Chief of Naval Operations. Following military service and a second

career as an investment banker, Grojean became the executive director of the Admiral Nimitz Foundation in Fredericksburg, Texas. Obituary, *San Antonio Express-News*, December 30, 2008, accessed through Ancestry.com, https://www.legacy.com/obituaries/sanantonio/obituary.aspx?n=charles-d-grojean-chuck&pid=121963380, February 26, 2019.

2. Stead Air Force Base began in 1942 as the Reno Army Airfield and was later named for Croston Stead, a flight training casualty. During the Cold War, it served as a center for intensive survival training, utilizing the harsh surrounding terrain for field maneuvers. Among those who trained at the installation were members of all military branches, as well as early US astronauts. In 1966 the base transferred to the City of Reno and transitioned as the Reno-Stead Airport. "History of Reno-Stead Airport," https://renoairport.com/airport-authority/reno-stead-airport-rts/history-reno-stead-airport, accessed February 26, 2019.

Bibliography

Barton, Augustus G. "LeMay Speaks Out." Privately published pamphlet. Newark: n.p., 1979.

Coffey, Thomas M. *Iron Eagle. The Turbulent Life of General Curtis LeMay*. New York: Crown Publishers, 1986.

Laur, Timothy M., and Norman Polmar, eds. *Strategic Air Command: People, Aircraft and Missiles*, 2nd ed. Baltimore: Nautical and Aviation Publishing Company of America, 1990.

McCombs, Don, and Fred L. Worth. *World War II: 4,139 Strange and Fascinating Facts*. New York: Wings Books, 1983.

McHenry, Robert, ed. *Webster's American Military Biographies*. Springfield, MA: G. & C. Merriam Company, 1978.

Nalty, Bernard C., ed. *Winged Shield, Winged Sword: A History of the United States Air Force, 1950–1997*, vol. 2. Washington, DC: Air Force History and Museums Program, 1997.

Parrington, Alan J. "Mutually Assured Destruction Revisited," *Airpower Journal*, Winter 1997, 4–19.

Peacock, Lindsay T. *Strategic Air Command*. London: Arms & Armour Press, 1988.

Snyder, Louis L. *Historical Guide to World War II*. Westport, CT: Greenwood Press, 1997.

"USAF 2015 Almanac," *Air Force Magazine*. Washington: Air Force Association, 2015.

Wagner, Ray. *American Combat Planes*. Garden City, NY: Doubleday, 1982.

Index

Note: Photo page numbers shown in *italics*

Abbott, Spenser, 97
Aggressor Force, 71–72
Air National Guard, 41, 79
Air Training Command, 29, 31
Air Transport Command, 88
Aircraft:
    707, 81
    B-17, 42, 96
    B-25, Mitchell bomber, 21, 25–29, 36
    B-29 Superfortress, 2, 43
    B-36, Peacemaker, 6–7, 25, 69
    B-47, 5, 8, 37–38, 40, 42–43, *57–59*, 69, 78
    B-50, 2, 6, 25
    B-52, 69
    Boeing, 8
    C-47, Gooney Bird, 25, 72
    C-119, Flying Coffin, 79
    C-124, 31, 88
    DC-3, 25
    Enola Gay, 36
    KC-97, Stratocruiser, 7–8, 25, *57–59*, 61, 79–81, 88, 92
    KC-135, 8, 81
    P-47, 2, 7
    P-51, 2
    Piper Cub, 21
    T-29, Flying Classroom, 25, 32, *54*
    T-36, 37

aircraft commander, 44–46, 81–82, 87–88, 89
Aircraft Identification Zones (ADIZ), 82, 88–89
Alexander, Capy Kromer, 35, 93–94, 98
Alexander, Edward Clifton, 10–11, 14, 16
Alexander, Gretchen, 14
Alexander, Ireanus "Rene" Morse, 12
Alexander, John, 12
Alexander, Richard "Dick," 10, 14, 17–18, 23
Alexander, Ruth Ethlyn Massey, 10–11
Alexander, TX, 93
Alexander, Thomas E., *48, 49, 50, 56*, 97–102
Alexander, William, 13
Allied Stores, 92
Amarillo Army Airfield, 38
American Legion, 19–94
American Military University, 93–94

Baylor University, 27
Beeman, Cynthia, 95
bombs (atomic, hydrogen, practice), 36–37
Bolling Field, Washington, DC, 2–3
Brize Norton air base, England, 41–42, 62, 76

Caldwell, Shirley, 95, 100
Carswell Air Force Base, 7
celestial navigation, 67–68

Index

Chillicothe, MO, 12
Churchill, Winston, 1
circular error, 37, 70, 80
Cleveland, Bill, 85–87
Clovis AFB, NM, 23
Coffey, Thomas M., 2
Cold War, 4–7, 9, 34, 43, 82–83, 100,102
Colorado State University, 61
Connally Air Force Base, Waco, TX, 27–28, 31
Cour d'Alene, ID, 14
Cuban missile crisis, 83, 84–90, 91

Daley, Richard "Dick," 91
Daughters of the American Revolution, 12
dead reckoning, 33
Desert Hot Wells, TX, 74
DeVore, Mr., 32
drum and bugle corps, 20

Eglin Air Force Base, FL, 23
Eisenhower, Dwight, 8, 79
Ellington Air Force Base (Ellington Field), Houston, TX, 24–25, 31, 43, 61, 69
Elmendorf, AK, 78
England, 34, 39, 41, 60–65

Falun, KS, 44–46
Farallon Islands, 88
flight evaluation board,
Ford, Barbara, 20
Fort Riley, KS, 20
Fort Worth, TX, 25, 36
French Air Force, 65

Galveston, TX, 24–25
Germany, 65
Goose Bay, Labrador, 39
Grant, Ulysses S., 4
Greenland, 39,78
Grojean, Charles "Chuck," 68–69

Harlingen, TX, 61
Hensley Naval Air Station, 92
Hickam Field, HI, 86–88
Hiroshima, Japan, 4
Hitler, Adolf, 1
Hofheinz, Roy, 67
Homestead Air Force Base, FL, 85, 90
Hondo Air Force Base, Hondo, TX, 62

Iceland, 63
IFF (identify friend or foe), 42
Illinois Air National Guard, 78–80
interrogation training, 71–74
Ireland, 34–35, 62

James, Jesse, 12–13
Joske's, 92

Kansas State College (Kansas State University), Manhattan, KS, 19–20
Kelly Field, TX, 88
Kennedy, John F., 84, 91
Kenney, George C., 2, 29, 65

Lee, Light Horse Harry, 12
LeMay, Curtis Emerson, 2–7, 8–9, 14, 28–30, 31, 34–35, 44, 46–47, 51, 52, 53, 65–67, 72, 77, 79, 99–100
Long Beach, CA, 10–11
Lowry Field, Denver, CO, 21, 83

MacArthur, Douglas, 2,29
Magee, John Gillespie, Jr., 21
March Air Force Base, Riverside, CA, 31–32
Marcus, Stanley, 92, 99–100
Marrowbone, KY, 12
Marshall Field (store), 78, 81, 83, 92
Massey, Mary Ann Hastings, 12–13
mathematics in navigation, 32, 62, 80
Maxwell Field, AL, 2
McCain, John, 71
McDevitt, Jack, 97

Military Air Transport Service, 31
Military aircraft. *See* Aircraft.
mole hole, 5, 37–38
Morocco, 63, 65
Munday, Major, 77
Museum of the Pacific War, Fredericksburg, TX, 14, 69
mutually-assumed destruction (MAD), 4–5, 83, 90

Nagasaki, Japan, 4
National Guard, 79–80, 84, 92
Nau, John L., III, 95, 100
Navasota, TX, 26
Neiman Marcus, 92–93, 95, 98
Nimitz, Chester, 10
Norden bombsight, 28–29, 36
North Atlantic Treaty Organization (NATO), 60, 76
North Pole, 38

Offutt Air Force Base, Omaha, NE, 3, 51, 77–78
Ohio State University, 3
Olson, Dale, 80–81
O'Leary, Joseph John, 64

parachuting, 43–45
Patton, George S., 1
Pearl Harbor, HI, 9, 14, 87
Perry, Rick, 94–95
Port Aransas, TX, 36
Pueblo, CO, 14, 20

radar, 32, 34, 39, 41, 70, 81–82, 86
Randolph Air Force Base, San Antonio, TX, 31
Rantoul, IL, 80–81
refueling, 8, 28, 40–43, 56–58, 78, 80
Reno, NV, 71
Reserve Officers Training Corps (ROTC), 3, 19–21, 22, 23, 66, 92
Rice Institute (Rice University), 32

Rio Vista, TX, 10
Royal Air Force (RAF), 60, 62, 65, 76

San Antonio Conservation Society, 95
sextant, 67–68
Sharpsteen, Duely, 19
Sherman, Walter, 42, 50, 61–64
Sherman, William Tecumseh, 4
Sidi Slimane Air Base, 63, 65
Smoky Hill Air Force Base, Salina, KS, 32, 35, 37, 39, 44–46, 56, 61, 64
Sons of the American Revolution, 12
Soviet Union (Soviets), 1, 4–6, 8, 35, 38, 62, 66, 82, 84, 90
Spaatz, Carl, 2–3, 8
spot promotions, 44
standboard officers, 37
Stalin, Josef, 1
Stead Air Force Base, 71, 73
Strategic Air Command (SAC), 2–7, 8–9, 28–29, 31–39, 40–47, 50, 51, 54, 60–66, 67–75, 76–83, 84, 90, 96, 99–100, 102
Strategic Air Command (the movie), 41
survival training, 72–74

Tactical Air Command (TAC), 34
tankers, 5, 8, 38, 41–42, 78, 88
Texas A&M College (Texas A&M University), 77, 79
Texas Capitol, 55, 96
Texas Historical Commission, 69, 95, 97, 100
Thule, Greenland, 77
Tokyo, Japan, 4, 9
Topeka, KS, 10
Travis Air Force Base, CA 85, 88, 89
Trondheim, Norway, 76

unconditional warfare, 4
University of Colorado, Boulder, CO, 20, 22, 61, 98
US Air Force, 2, 8, 14, 22, 28, 61, 80

US Air Force (and US Army Air Force) units:
    40th Bombardment Wing, 32, 61, 78
    108th Refueling Squadron, 78
    305th Bombardment Group, 3
    Eighth Air Force, 30
    Fifth Air Force, 29
    Twentieth Air Force, 3
US Army, 66
US Army Air Corps Flying School, 3
US Army Air Forces, 2, 28
US Army Reserve, 3
US Army Signal Corps, 10
US Military Academy. *See* West Point.
US Navy, 10
US Strategic Forces, 3
Utley, Dan K., *56*, 95

Vietnam (Vietnamese), 9, 27, 86
Virginia, Alexandria, 13
Vladivostok, Soviet Union, 34

Wake Island, 43, 84–85, 87–88, 90
Wayne, John, 27, 93, 99–100
weather ships, 39
Wellington, KS, 10, 14–16, 18–19, 69
West Point, 3, 66
Wichita, KS, 16
World War I, 10
World War II (and World War II-era aircraft), 1, 4, 6, 10, 13–14, 16–17, 25–26, 32, 35, 37–38, 42–43, 64, 69–70, 76, 81, 95, 96, 100; scrap drives in, 17